D1606087

NEW PASTOR
NEW PARISH

Discovering Parish Perils… and Pearls

Reflections on entry and engagement in parish ministry

Thoughts on surviving or thriving…

JAMES G. COBB

Wipf & Stock Publishers
Eugene, Oregon

Wipf & Stock Publishers
199 West 8th Avenue, Suite 3
Eugene, OR 97401

New Pastor, New Parish

ISBN: 1-59752-126-4
Publication Date: April 2005

10 9 8 7 6 5 4 3 2 1

Dedication

To Judy, Chris and Stephen Cobb who lived these "episodes"
in ministry and with special appreciation for Judy's insights
as a clergy colleague in ministry.

Special thanks to Lutheran Theological Seminary at Gettysburg
for encouragement to teach and write this manuscript;
to Barbara and Ken Link for editing assistance, and to the manuscript
readers including those special and helpful persons on the book cover!

About the author...

The Rev. Dr. James G. Cobb is Assoc. Dean for Church Vocations and Lifelong Learning at Lutheran Theological Seminary at Gettysburg. He has served parishes in Annapolis, Md., Fredericksburg, Va., Grand Rapids, Mi. and 1988-99, First Lutheran Church, Norfolk, Va. During his tenure as pastor in Norfolk, a published book underwritten by the Lilly Foundation identified his congregation in Norfolk as one of the "300 Most Excellent Protestant Parishes in the U.S.," cited as one of 20 among E.L.C.A. Lutherans. Pastor Cobb has served on the E.L.C.A. Church Council for 8 years; the E.L.C.A. Study on Ministry (1988-93), and on the national church's Ecumenical Advisory Committee, 1993-2001. He was part of the church's ecumenical visitation group to Geneva, London, Strasbourg, Rome and Istanbul for conversations with world leaders including the Pope and Patriarchate in 1995 and, in 1997, was an E.L.C.A. delegate to Lutheran World Federation Assembly in Hong Kong. Pastor Cobb is married to the Rev. Judith A. Cobb, Coordinator for Region 8, E.L.C.A. and they are the parents of two sons. Pastor Cobb has authored sermon books, plays and magazine articles. The most recent include a book of sermons, "Sermonic City Sidewalks," (1999) and a chancel drama play about Martin and Katie Luther, "Reformation's Rib." (2001). Called to the Seminary's staff in 1999, he serves in various capacities including Admissions, Church Relations, Continuing Education for laity and clergy, (serves as Director for "Summer Institute" and "Lay School of Theology") and is a regular seminary newsletter and synodical columnist throughout Region 8. Pastor Cobb has chaired seminary committees for Youth Ministry Certification School and the recently obtained Lilly Grant for work with youth and vocational discernment.

Table of Contents

Foreword ix

CALL COMMITTEES 1

ENTRY INTO THE NEW PARISH 9
Pre-entry information 9
Gathering information 10
Judicatory officials 10
Networking 10

Those first days 11
Parish transitions: 11
About Crisis Ministry 12
About Preaching 13
About Graciousness 14
About "paying the dues" 14
About planning 15
About referral systems 16
About yellow blinking lights 17
About visitation 18

Nuts and bolts of parish administration 24
Parish constitution 26
The budget 26
The parish register 26
The congregational climate 27
Communications 28
Stewardship 29
The budget and the pastor 31
Continuing stewardship matters 32
Watch out warnings 33
Specialities 34
Expectations of committees 35
Decision making in the church 37
Congregational meetings and the constitution 38
Varieties of "land mines: 39
About music and choirs 40
Missed assumptions about the pastor 41
Pastoral reporting 42
Committees in the parish 42

Surprises in ministry ... 44
Gratitude is missing ... 45
Weddings ... 45
Wisdom ... 46

Other considerations ... 49
Personal pastoral qualities ... 49
Graciousness ... 50
Discretion ... 50
Restraint ... 51
Appearance/demeanor ... 51
Thoughtfulness ... 52
Hospitality ... 52

Priesthood of all believers ... 54

Most Excellent congregations ... 57

CHURCH FIGHTS/FIGHTING FAIR ... 59
Pastoral Ministry Life Savers ... 65
Colleague helpers (mutual ministry, peer groups, mentors) ... 66
Time management ... 66
Lifelong learning ... 67

APPENDIX A ... 69
Clerical collar as "gift and sign"

APPENDIX B ... 72
Calculating "household income equivalents"

APPENDIX C ... 74
10 Commandments of "vacancy etiquette"

APPENDIX D ... 76
Pastoral check-list upon arriving at a new parish

APPENDIX E ... 80
Congregational check-list for "Welcoming a New Pastor"

APPENDIX F ... 83
Sample form for monthly pastoral report to church councils

Foreword

A new friend, Tony Aguilar, Assistant to the Bishop, Metro New York Synod, once said this: "ministry is messy." Of course it is. We just don't think about that so much. Ministry is not so much about "getting things right," as it a matter of taking the journey, walking/talking the adventure called faith with a particular people called, not by us, but by God, to be fellow pilgrims on the way. Pastors are not comparable to engineers who build structures according to "specs," but are more like artists. The parish is a canvas where some things are already drawn in, or are outlined or are full- blown pictures here and there. Now, the new pastor steps forward to add to the picture. What will be created? How will some new pictures take shape? What special chemistries come together? In the end, God will put the whole cosmic/historic/mysterious mosaic in place. In the meantime….we are there. What will be shaped?

What I offer in these following pages are not specs about ministry, not a "how to" manual but a reflection on a journey that I have been privileged to walk in parish ministry. I think there is some humor and some help and lots of hope offered in these pages. Where your experience says "Yes, I know that!" then some truth is relayed. Where you experience an 'ah ha' moment of reflection, great!

And where you say, "No way," take part in the great debate about how we all take different avenues while we journey together as followers of *"The Way."* I do hope the readings and reflections help in parish ministry. It is a great place to serve, lead, preach, teach, worship and work. I do acknowledge that what I have written is biographical hence, the words about marriage, spouse and family, but I hope single colleagues may yet glean some insights from such excursions. I am also aware that various ethnic specific ministries will have special foci (e.g., in Latino congregations, a clerical collar is much more mandatory than optional (appendix A). All parishes and pastors have specific "social locations" for ministry. With these caveats, may each reader be renewed, refreshed and uplifted as on eagle's wings…

CALL COMMITTEES:

Pulpit or call committees are formed during vacancies and most congregations are given strict guidelines about who is on them, how they are selected, etc. If one is well coached by judicatory officials, one will know what they may ask and what may be inappropriate. They will be urged to keep strict confidences about who is interviewed but this may not be done because there are simply too many people in the know: i.e., judicatory officials, colleagues, local council or officers, spouses, people who happen to see the candidate at the interview site who may know the person, etc. But, the attempt is made to try to keep things secret.

In my 28 years of ministry, I can count approximately 40 phone call inquiries or contacts asking about my interest in other calls. That averages more than one a year and many could be handled with a simple "no" after an initial phone call. The timing was wrong, too early in a new call, etc. But usually, I think that a pastor must at least listen to the inquiry (they are all serious from the other church's standpoint) and look at the materials. Since there is no ideal time for tenure, an exploration of a call situation may occur even in relatively short tenures if there is a seeming match between gifts and needs. In the Church, there must be space for the Holy Spirit to work. In initial contacts, there will be a real sense of both flattery and ego-stroking but neither will be enough for the ministry tasks should you accept the new call. Other things must be considered. The image of call committees is still the image of "dating" with the possibility of marriage. How awkward these times are. Still, many questions from the prospective pastor need to be kept in mind.

IN YOUR HEAD...

First, remember that the call committee is on the prowl for the "perfect pastor." You may be familiar with this anonymous but funny quip about "perfect pastors": "After hundreds of fruitless years, model pastors have been developed that will suit everyone. It is guaranteed that they will please any church that calls them. They preach exactly 14 minutes and then sit down. They condemn sin but never hurt anyone's feelings. They work from 8 AM to 10 PM in every type of endeavor from preaching to custodial services. They make $100. a week, wear good clothes, buy good books, have a nice family, drive a fine car and give $50. a week to the church. They also stand ready to contribute to every good cause with which they are confronted. They are 28 years old and have been preaching for 35 years. They are tall/short, thin/heavyset, and nice looking. They have one brown eye and one blue. Hair is parted in the middle, left side is dark and straight, the right side is light and wavy. They have a burning desire to work with youth and spend all their time with older folks. They smile all the time. They always work with a straight face because of their sincerity and they have a sense of humor that keeps them seriously dedicated to their work. They make 25 calls a day on church members, spend all their time evangelizing the un-churched, visit all the inactive members and are always available at the office. What's more, they give to every organization and group in the church and the community, they give total leadership, and never discourage the initiative of the laity." Therefore, the first myth to dispel is the thought of perfection. We aren't the perfect pastors and there are no perfect congregations. Let's say that aloud and get over it.

ON THE PHONE...

So much of how a committee presents its congregation depends on its own homework and preparation. I have heard committees that obviously have come together for the first time at the interview! Ask them a question and they may get into an argument with each other about history or programs or who does what. (Not a good moment to experience). On the phone, it is good for you to ask these two things:

1.) Will they interview multiple persons or will you be interviewed and then told rather quickly, "Yes, we wish to continue with you," or, "Thank you, but we wish to continue our process for some time?"
2.) What is their time line for decision making and when would they hope to conclude their process?

So much of a pastor's thoughts, energies and reflections will be expended on entering the "day-dreaming field" of a new call that a lingering six month's investment in waiting/hoping versus a two week window of consideration, is worth your knowing from the beginning as to how it will be.

Ask about the kind of process they envision.

- Will they first visit your congregation on a Sunday?

- Do they wish to receive any materials from you?
- Will the interview/meeting be at your place or theirs?
- Is there an expected involvement of spouse at some point?
- How might an information flow between pastor and congregation take place?

Any preparatory information between the pastor and the call committee is helpful.

FACE-TO-FACE...

Introductions are so important. They are ice-breakers but also set a tone. You are nervous and so are they. They have been entrusted with a major congregational assignment: to find the pastor for their church! You are entrusted with a major life decision: Is this a call where God wishes me to be? If you need to take some notes, do so. Especially important are the names of the committee members. Hopefully, it will not be a group larger than 8 and trying to remember the names quickly (and use them) is very important. Even if this is not one of your talents, it will serve you well to remember the committee members' names during the conversations. Seminary students have asked me in class a series of interesting questions about call committees, and this has given me an opportunity to remember. I share some of these remembrances with you because they form a basis for some commentary. First, call committees are composed of some interesting types. Here are some examples:

- ***The theological inquiry panel.*** Some think their chief and primary goal is to serve as a church "truth squad" to weed out heresy. Many do not realize that you went through faculty and examining panels to get to this point and this is not their duty. But, it usually means that a parishioner has some axe to grind and wants to inquire about your understanding of Bible, miracles, social activism, abortion, gay/lesbian issues, virgin birth, etc. You've probably had enough practice at these probes to respond well. If not, get in some practice sessions with colleagues! While pastors may be irritated at where such conversations lead, they must articulate clearly their understanding of the church's statement on these matters, and, from the committee's viewpoint, it is fair to expect to hear such articulation from a pastoral candidate.
- ***Pastoral "clone" committee.*** Some think that they are on the committee to get someone who most closely resembles the last pastor. Genetic cloning holds great promise for such persons. If you get a glimpse of the last pastor's picture or know their personality, you may wonder how alike or different you are. It may be an advantage

for the pastor to probe at what this committee thinks the last pastor's priorities, emphases, strengths and weaknesses were in order to determine what may be in store for the congregation's next chapter. Beware of comparisons, good or bad. How shall you help to teach that you are your own unique individual person while continuing to be one of the "called of God" in the congregation's stream of history?

- ***"Turf protectors":*** Some think they wish the new pastor to know quickly, even in initial interviews, that there are some "sacred cows" not to be touched; there are some turfs in certain parishioners protective custody to be safe from the world and from the pastor. It may be the altar guild or the music program or the sacramental practices or a Sunday school class or a room in the building, but there will be some "turfs" not welcoming of newcomers and not welcoming of any administrative interference (that means you). You may as well probe such boundaries and get a feel for the "lay of the land" early on.
- ***Miracle workers:*** Some are on the committee to find the one whose ideas and gifts will be just the right thing needed to fix the church's problems. They will say, "For years now, we have looked for a pastor to lead us in_________." You are on the spot. What will you do about their problems, hopes and dreams? Usually, it's a sure bet that one of these areas will be the need: growth in numbers (couched in the word "evangelism"); stewardship (unfortunately, this usually means that they haven't made their budget in years); youth ministry (everyone thinks it's the pastor's job and what do you think?) and Christian Education (meaning, we are all burned out, have all taught for 20 years and we need a break…HELP!). And so it goes. When you do not become the committee's primary candidate, remember please that Jesus would have had a tough time here too.
- ***"Soul mates."*** Some committee members want to get in touch with the candidate's "inner feelings" to be sure the emotional landscape is healthy and well adjusted and will be "empathetic" with parishioners' feelings. I remember a person on one call committee asked me to share with the committee when I last cried. I replied that I chose to share that kind of detail with whomever I wished to share it and that didn't include this group whom I had just met a few minutes before. I never heard from them again. Touchy/feely people are around and wish to draw pastors into the arena of feelings and emotions even if we don't wish to go there. Clinical pastoral education has probably given good preparation for such conversations.
- ***Saints and elders:*** Most committees will have someone in the group who represents the older members and the history repository of the congregation. Such elders have seen the church live through various cycles and turns and may help steady the group in taking its time,

looking beyond a "pretty face" or an ugly one to see the substance of who a person is. Such ones have a wealth of experience, wisdom and tenacity to "stay the course" in pastoral selection processes. Listen to the wisdom and the depth of their memories, hurts and hopes. Their words may bring forth prophetic utterances of truth-telling and kingdom yearnings so straight and on target that you are helped and blessed all at once!

GETTING R.E.A.L... Call committees are about these things:

1.) ***Relationships:*** get to know the committee. Be active in listening to pick up clues about each person's hopes and dreams about their congregation. They are trying to get a take on your personality to determine whether there is good chemistry for a match. Enjoy them as people and for the perspectives they bring and represent as a slice of the congregation. You may only have one session with these people, so consider it an adventure and treat it that way. Should you not go forward, there will still be learnings gleaned from such encounters that will serve you well in the future.
2.) ***Education:*** gather all the information possible about the congregation: its trends over the last five years, its unique problems and struggles. You need to know all you can glean from annual reports, newsletters and conversations committee members will share. Don't be hesitant in asking questions. Do they offer good disclosure or do they sugar-coat their problems?
3.) ***Analysis:*** the information gathered may point you to issues and trajectories for the next five years. If you can clearly see what they hope and need and can be true about your gifts and talents and interests in taking on such a congregation, well and good. If not, it would be good for you to express a need to withdraw from consideration as a candidate. Analysis is very much about attempts to match "needs" with "gifts." All partners need honest conversation for such to happen.
4.) ***Living arrangements:*** information should be shared about parsonage/housing allowance; exploration of the setting of the parish and its context for ministry need to be explored; the family's well-being with schools and community will be part of the conversation. Does a church have an office or study? Are there staffing arrangements and if so, are they paid or volunteer? How would this committee speak of the community's strengths and weaknesses? Why would they hope you would move here? (More about this in the chapter on "entry and transitions.")

Following a call committee meeting, it is common courtesy to write a note thanking the committee for their hospitality (meals/lodging/hosting, etc.) and reiterating once again, your understanding that the committee will make a decision immediately or within a specified time.

FANTASY LAND...

There are things I wish had happened over the years that didn't.

I wish that I could have been locked alone for an afternoon inside the church building. I would have stood in the chancel to imagine leading worship and looked at the pulpit to wonder if that was a place where I should stand. I would have roamed the halls looking at bulletin boards to see what issues and invitations were before the people of God. I would have looked at classrooms to think about the children and their environment for learning the stories of Jesus. I would have gotten an impression of how the congregation thought of its building as a home and as a tool for ministry in their care (or lack of care) for a holy place.

I wish I could see their worship on Sunday to see if faces were involved, excited and joyous or bored and burdened. I would see how they worship with grace or with awkward uncertainty. I would see if the pews were filled or empty and whether the hair was all silver or mixed and whether it was quiet like a museum or noisy as a nursery. I would see if they welcomed a stranger or ignored me. I would listen to their prayers as if invited into their passions or their passivity- which?

I wish I might meet some of their children and see if they loved their church, its safety and adventure and leaders. I would like to see if they knew and "owned" the building. I'd like to see if adults frowned at them or paid attention to them. I would like to know if they love Jesus.

I wish I could roam the immediate neighborhood and ask neighbors, store clerks and passersby, "Do you know anything about this church?" What's it like? What's its reputation? Does it matter if it's here today, gone tomorrow? Is there some sense of pride in the neighborhood; is it a place in desperate need of the church? Is the land neighborly or is it enemy terrain?

I wish I could find one honest and devoted Christian disciple who knew me and the congregation so intimately that they could say directly, "You need to offer/take this call and serve here." But that's just too great a fantasy.

Speaking of great fantasies, consider Ryan Ahlgrim's and Randy Roth's humorous composition:

"The top ten statements pastors would like to hear...

10. Hey, it's my turn to sit in the front pew!
9. I was so enthralled, I never noticed the sermon went overtime by 20 minutes.
8. Personally, I find witnessing more enjoyable than golfing.
7. Pastor, I've decided to give our church the $500. a month I used to send to the TV evangelists.
6. I volunteer to be the permanent Sunday School teacher for the middle school class.
5. Forget the synod guidelines, let's pay our pastor a good living wage.
4. I love it when we sing hymns we've never sung before.
3. Since we're already here, let's start the worship service early.
2. Pastor, we'd like to send you to that Bible seminar in the Bahamas.
1. Nothing inspires me and strengthens my commitment like the annual business meeting."

So, call committees and pastors sometimes do get beyond fantasy land to actual calls, many of them working well. How did that happen? What is involved finally in getting a match made?

- Prayer and reflection go into overdrive during this time. You will find that you wrestle with two calls: a call to stay and a call to go, a call to say yes and a call to say no (some variation on this if it is a seminarian's first call). Prayers intensify. Conversations with trusted colleagues sketch out different scenarios.
- If you are married and/or have children, spouse and family considerations enter the arena with intense engagement. Family members will have great emotional involvement in every decision. Even the quiet ones who seem to have no opinion may be churning with emotions under the surface. Some family members may be rooted types who will see a move as "death and dying," great loss of place, friends, schools, and all sorts of comfort zones. Others may be persons who consider the whole thing a great adventure full of excitement and anticipation. There are types who are ready to stay and types who are ready to roll! The debate within the family will intensify. There may be great anguished arguments, quiet sobbing, emotions of grief or even betrayal. There may be times of great affirmation and anticipation. The spouse may experience loss of friends, perhaps employment and the familiar circles of community. This is a major moment to minister to one another, to hold each other in an embrace of caring, listening, sharing, expressing losses and fears as well as hopes for the new place and people. This will be the single most important consideration in the whole matter of a new call. And it

may be the one least addressed by congregations, judicatory officials and sadly, our own family members. Much work and attention needs to be focused here regardless of the time and energy it takes. Is there someone you can all identify (another pastor/friend, conference Dean or a counselor/parishioner...after the matter becomes public... who might be invited over for an evening and who can go around the family and ask how each thinks of the upcoming change? Is there a way to have a structured meeting around such a conversation while keeping it informal in the home? The benefits would be helpful and might help to clarify issues and feelings). There is never too much attention paid to the family unit on this matter. Sadly, there is often too little. Such matters are not concluded when the moving van leaves the new house. In fact, the need to listen and watch and pay attention will continue. All sensitivity is needed for the ones you love.

- Your gut will be wrenched with the mind's picture painting as you give consideration to a new call. How would it be there, in that new place? What new chapters are yet to be written where I am? Are there signs? Am I open to a guidance that moves me towards a new call and new people and place of ministry? We are a people with great hindsight and very little foresight. How shall I know?

Questions for reflection:

1. How do you know how to decide about the call you are in and the call you are considering? What is most important to you in the reflection time?
2. What do you wish you had done differently "once-upon-a-time" in your considerations?
3. What advice/insights can you offer to new pastors embarking on such new territory?
4. What do you feel are the honesty levels of call committees? What have been your experiences?
5. What are the needs of the family through the time of a move?

ENTRY INTO THE NEW PARISH:

It is with fear and trembling that one enters upon a new call in parish ministry. What to do? How to prioritize? Where to begin? These are questions each new pastor must answer. Without any training most pastors learn by "trial and error." Our own personalities and interests become a guide. Often, we follow our inclinations, instincts and personal wishes. In spite of such leadings, there are some bases that do need to be covered. The following are offered as guideposts along the way:

NECESSARY "PRE-ENTRY," INFORMATION:

Obviously, as many materials as possible, should be gathered during the call interview process.

INFORMATION GATHERING:

A. Included in the packet which any congregation should send are these: constitution, annual report (perhaps two, at five year intervals); budget (if not included in the annual report), mission statement, congregational history, bulletins from a couple of festival worship services and a couple of "ordinary" Sundays, pictures of the facility, pictures of offices and parsonage (if one is offered), pictorial directory, long range plan (should one exist), pertinent brochures on special programs (pre-school, evangelism pamphlets, etc.), job descriptions of all staff members (very important) and the understandings by the church council of their continuance or terminations (i.e, how shall this be determined and agreed to by pastor and parish council?). And now the obvious: read the materials! Do the research. You are making every effort to discover their real expectations and attempting to state yours as clearly and as succinctly as possible.

Reason: You are gathering information. You would like to see trends. You would like to know what the mission, history and priorities of the congregation seem to be over time.

B. Conversation with the appropriate judicatory official. This may be the Bishop or the Bishop's assistant who deals directly with the vacant parish council and call committee. A face-to-face sit down session is essential. In the conversation these topics should be addressed:
   - the history of the parish (strengths and weaknesses, heartaches and hopes)
   - assessment of your gifts and talents and interests and why the Bishop believes you might be considered (in other words, "Why me and not some other 'warm body?")
     (Pay attention to the synod's response to the two questions above because one would hope to receive helpful information and insights).
   - Ask the Bishop what his/her hopes and ministry direction for this parish would be in the future.
   - Ask the Bishop what his/her involvement/visitation with you and the parish might be through your tenure (i.e., is it only "crisis intervention" or structured visitation or nothing?)
   - Can the judicatory official request during the vacancy that three things be addressed by the official and the parish council: 1. a membership audit (to see that rolls and parish register are updated and accurate); 2. a personnel/staff audit (job descriptions in place and what understandings have been reached with continuing staff concerning their continuance or resignations); 3. a financial audit of all accounts (to ensure proper procedures and accountabilities. This should be done during the vacancy so that it is not the "new pastor's" distrust of persons and/or procedures).

Reason: You will get an idea of how much and how supportive the denominational officials will work with you through the vacancy. You will discover how much or how little they know about this parish, you and your potential future together. The side benefit is the establishment of a sense of "partnership" with judicatory church (a good thing to know and have).

C. Other networking: (understood to be confidential if you are a potential candidate for the pastorate: make it clear):
   - Are there or should there be conversations with the former pastor (s)?
   - Can you make opportunities to speak with neighboring pastors both of your denomination and other denominations, especially

asking about collegiality in social ministries/ecumenical endeavors, etc.?

- Is there a trusted colleague with whom your confidential consideration of the call can be reflectively considered?

Reason: You are beginning to prayerfully consider a call. All conversations, information and relationships are vital to your considerations/deliberations and reflections.

Questions for Reflections:

1. How did you gather information about your perspective parish?
2. How helpful were judicatory officials in your discussion/reflection/consideration of your new call?
3. Will/can you discuss with them what was helpful and what you wish they had considered during the vacancy and during your reflection about the new call?

THOSE FIRST DAYS:

Personal Transitions:

It takes a while to unpack boxes and to get familiar books into their new niches. While you are attempting to get this done, there are many other concerns on your mind.

- It may be the happiness and well being and transition of a spouse and/or family.
- It may be grief and sadness at the departure from comfortable and familiar surroundings, close friends and a way of life.
- There are details simply about "transitions" that will take time: address changes to every credit card and mail forwarding (to every person known to God!), establishing new bank and insurance accounts, driver's licensing and car tags, a new doctor and dentist and all the attendant record transfers, settling children into a new house and a new neighborhood.
- The second circle of transition involves getting to know school systems, finding new hobbies and recreation and making new friends. Perhaps simply reading this list to a new church council will generate appropriate empathy with your first weeks of your "dizzy-headed energy drain." For some of us and spouses and children, the move is a "great adventure" which is anticipated, relished and enjoyed. For others the reaction can be severe trauma similar to death and dying. No one knows when each of these extremes will manifest itself in which person and at what time! Life in a new place will swing between the emotions of death and resurrection and its gradual ending is imprecise. Please know, however, that no one in your family is immune. Be aware and considerate.

Parish Transitions:

Your first days will involve the above emotions but in the parish there will also be these immediate dynamics:

A. ***About Crisis Ministry:*** Yes, things happen to people even in inopportune times. In one parish, the funeral of the congregation's 'matriarch' occurred in the first month. It was an interesting dynamic. Everyone wanted to be helpful for the 'new pastor.' After all, he did not know her.

   People came to share stories and this was helpful. But there were rather direct hints that the pastor emeritus ought to have a part in the funeral. How can this be handled? This vignette offers two points for reflection.

   1. First, the listening to stories is great! I think the biographies of parishioners are fascinating. Each person is unique as a special child of God. Listen to the stories. Listen well. Those stop-in moments by several in the congregation were helpful and I acknowledged the stories and the help in the funeral meditation.
   2. Listen to this truth: You will forever "shadow box" with former pastors and you cannot win anything here for they are officially "saints of blessed memory." Acknowledge this, but do not succomb to it. So, in the case of the funeral, I heard the requests and dealt with them in this way: Indeed, it would be good if the former pastor could take a part, and so I extended the invitation to read the lessons but not to preach. The pastor, called and installed, is charged with the preaching office. Hopefully, former pastors ought (from any sense of ministerial ethics) to say to such requests from parishioners or present pastor, "Thank you, I would love to come and worship but as a parishioner in the pew.") Not surprisingly, however, the flattery, the pastor's own ego and the grieving appeal of close friends and parishioners make this sentence rather difficult to utter.
   3. Therefore, I am most protective of the <u>present</u> pastor's role in preaching and ministry. It is <u>this</u> pastor to whom the family must turn and relate for pastoral care. It is <u>this</u> pastor who builds and solidifies relationships by being the pastor in such crisis times. Of course, a new pastor has not the knowledge, background, tenure and friendships that a former pastor has enjoyed. However, the present pastor builds these in the heat of crisis and times of need.

   Other crisis times provide these opportunities: the sudden emergency room visit with parishioners, the still-born baby, the shock of a suicide, the crash of an automobile, a devastating diagnosis, a grandparent's sudden death, a child's broken bone, the call from a funeral home. Each and every crisis in its "kairos" moment is the place where the gospel of grace alone suffices. The pastor, by presence and by word, is communicator of God's loving embrace in that time and in that event. The pastor is trained, formed and sent forth to embody that grace, speak the prayers, hold the hands and offer the Gospel's comfort to the broken, pained and drained people of God who are numbed and shocked and who feel so abandoned. It is not a former pastor's role or office so to do. It is yours. Even through the crisis, the relationship of pastor and people is made special. Thus, you are forever remembered as the pastor who came and saw, grieved and spoke, and consoled and comforted. This is your calling. "Crisis" is that moment. Your first days will also involve...

B. *About Preaching...* The basic expectations for a pastor need to proceed in the first days, weeks and months with all the excellence you can offer. Pastors are surprised to find that the most awkward times in a new parish involve preaching. After all, we concentrate on preaching in our seminary education and in our parish calls. Therefore, we should be most adept at this in a new place? Right? No! We come to discover that we preach from within the community of God's people and in this time of new beginnings, we are "displaced persons." We are not sure of the issues, communal histories and stories of the people before whom we stand. So, one must preach standing in a new and unfamiliar place. In the first days/weeks/months the texts of Scripture will come alive with themes of "new beginnings, transitions and changes." We think all the concentration we expend as preachers is most important. But we do not yet know who our listeners are or what the issues of their life circumstances are. Thus, we may find ourselves "off balance" as a preacher for a while. An associate pastor with me in Michigan once served a congregation in an Ivy League town and had various theology professors in his congregation. One Sunday one of them came through and greeted him with the affirmation, "That was the best sermon on that text, I have ever heard." He felt good and affirmed. Five minutes later another came through and said, "My dear friend and pastor, what did that sermon have to do with anything?" It was then he knew that listeners brought something to the preaching task! As preachers in a new place, we may know a text, its illustrative possibilities and its well crafted form, but we do not yet know the listeners. Receive this "off balance" time as normal and do not panic. Pastor-parish relationships will come in time and preaching will be strengthened because of who and what we know as the 'listeners and doers of the Word.' Patience with yourself during this time.

C. *About "Graciousness"...* Consciously, our beginnings are so important in a new parish. Opportunities in preaching, worship planning and leadership, teaching, baptisms, funerals and weddings will be the most public times when a whole congregations looks on, leans in and 'gets with' the new pastor. Tones are most important. You've heard it before: It's not what we say but how we say that is so important. We pastors tend to work on the "head" dimension of our ministry when the parish is most responsive to the "heart" part of us and our styles of ministry. They will look and listen for welcome, hospitality, humor, graciousness, caring and compassion. They will hear with their hearts concerning matters of consolation and comfort, grace and mercy. The listing of St. Paul's "fruits of the Spirit," is the real inventory of early listening in a new congregation. Read Galatians 5: 22-24 and get the drift of the personable but very real listening channels which parishioners hope to hear in their time with pastors. Take heed. Remember: call committees and congregations don't care so much about how much you know but rather, they will attempt to sense how much you care. How shall this apply to the one's entry in a new ministry setting?

D. *About "paying the dues."* Another "paying the dues" may often come in things that will be done in the first year but not necessarily on a continuing basis. Examples include: public prayers, invocations and sermons. Nearly every new pastor is asked to pray at special events and civic meetings. It is an opportunity for public introduction of the newcomer and the rounds of these events may occur in the first year but not necessarily beyond. There are some weird and ticklish moments. I was once asked to speak a blessing for the new sprinkler system at a country club golf course. (I respectfully declined even though golf is dear to my heart! And I had to offer my member some conversations about why I declined.) In another setting I was asked to give an invocation and benediction at a state convention. I had no idea who the speaker would be. He was a former high ranking state government official whose speech blasted various minorities. I could have left the head table in protest. That was an option. Finally, at his conclusion as he returned to the audience, I asked all to stand, but not for the expected formal benediction but for a prayer of blessing upon departure. Taking all the groups he had slammed in his speech, I prayed for God's gracious kindness and upholding of such people. Was it a prophetic moment of a Gospel response? I do not know. The "discomfort" of civic religion may face each pastor upon entry into the public arena. Thoughts about how you will handle requests for inter-faith/generic prayers is a topic for Christians to consider and weigh before the requests come. Other "paying your dues" moments can include family events, anniversary groups, boy and girl scouts, etc.

Yet another matter so integral to new parish entry relates to youth in the congregation. Realize a couple of things: youth are usually the most conservative group in the parish and they too have grieved, often at the departure of the last pastor, but no one has given much attention to their thoughts and emotions. The new pastor is immediately in a "no win" situation with youth (especially senior highs). Pastors have learned that it takes almost three years (until those 10th graders graduate) before new patterns of youth ministry and a real switch-over in allegiances and relationships takes hold. Still, during entry weeks and months, if a pastor gives attention to youth and youth leaders, listens to their critiques, hurts and hopes, invites them into the office, greets and laughs with them, the sheer offers of your graciousness and thoughtfulness will help a great deal. Some pastors have gatherings of youth groups or grades at their home in order for the social and informal introductions to be made. Youth will appreciate your attention. You may still be seen as the "substitute teacher" who took Pastor so-and-so's place, but at least you've tried. It's worth the effort. Just don't expect a great warm response for your efforts.

E. ***About planning:*** Finally, in these early days/weeks and months ministry will involve not only crisis times and routine times but also planning times, and one should and ought to reflect and attempt to…

Watch, listen and laugh: So much of the first year will be a struggle of "sensitization" and discerning, also appropriate "de-sensitization." Let me illustrate the latter first. In one congregation there was a patriarchal usher who truly was a "doorkeeper in the house of the Lord." This was a man of good grace and humor and sparkle, but on my second Sunday in the parish he presented me with a gift of a new wrist watch. He said he noticed I did not have one. (True, the one I had was broken and not yet repaired). A gift is okay, but he said something about the congregation being used to "shorter sermons." Ouch! It was time to be de-sensitized and to do so with humor. I laughed. He laughed. I told him that my previous congregation had a large clock on the balcony overhang that could clearly be seen from the pulpit. And how I missed such a prop! Humor and de-sensitization were needed. Can you imagine a pastor who would receive such a gift or comment as an offensive remark and sarcastically or caustically reply? Yet, I have known colleagues who would have reacted that way. Humor, of the self-deprecating kind, will serve well in the entry stages of a new parish and will endear you to a congregation. Enjoy the banter!

A second illustration: It is good and useful to establish a "mutual ministry" committee early in a new tenure to get some of the "de-sensitizing" input. (Use denominational guides for such a group. I have always asked the Council to produce a large listing of persons who would be confidential, insightful and knowledgeable of the congregation. Each of these "job description" adjectives is important.) Once, in the first six months of a new pastorate, I received an anonymous letter from a parishioner with a scathing attack on my preaching and delivery style. I was devastated, slumped over, depressed. I raised the issue at the mutual ministry committee and began reading the letter. One of the members said, "Oh, that's so-and-so," she writes those letters every so often to every pastor about her issues. Forget it!" A ton of weight was lifted from my shoulders. The rest of the meeting went into preaching/styles/structures and became a wonderfully affirming conversation. My step was much lighter the next day. My sensitivity to a letter was de-sensitized by my "pastoral committee." I was grateful beyond words.

A third illustration: other "sensitization" moments come as you observe the workings of committees and all new groups that you meet. Is the chair in charge or do all members look to someone else for comment or decision? Who are the congregation's "tribal chiefs" and what are the turfs that certain people control? (Especially beware of choirs and altar guilds when considering proscribed "turfs." Tread with extra care and use precise teaching and information as to why your changes are being made).

A fourth illustration: Figure out the grapevine. After a time in a parish, one becomes aware too of the communication patterns of congregations, otherwise known as the "grapevine" (we are talking gossip here). It can be used for good. Some things said to the appropriate people can result in good communications too. A parishioner in a former parish told me recently that the new pastor (after six years) had just learned that if he told some news to two people in particular, it would be shared through the whole parish and that he had just begun to use such knowledge. Sensitization to communication patterns may help.

What about other strategies for the entry? Always include the following:

F. *About Referral Systems:* One of the pastor's lifelines will be the early network formed with colleagues in ministry. An early visitation goal ought to include your sisters and brothers in your denominational groupings and the local version of a ministerium with other pastors. I like to joke and say, "When you want to know about the neighborhood, ask the Roman Catholic priest. When you want to know about social ministry and cooperative/ecumenical ventures, ask the Methodist minister. For music, concerts, theater and great restaurants, ask your Episcopal colleague. For the local political scene or to get your best clergy tax accountant, ask the Presbyterian clergy." Forgive my stereotypes, but they haven't failed me yet. In addition, in each visit you should ask each pastor about the counselor/counseling agency which they most frequently use, and why. If a name or agency seems to re-appear, you might trust such a referral for your needs. Counseling referrals will probably begin to happen IMMEDIATELY in your tenure and your quick-study knowledge of such referrals is crucial. In addition, it is well worth a pastor's time to schedule meetings with persons such as counselors, police chief, newspaper editor, school superintendent and city manager and/or mayor/president of local borough or city municipality both as a courtesy call and as a fount of information about the context of your ministry. In each parish I have served I have especially sought out the news reporter who covers religion. Such personal relationships have proved beneficial when checking on denominational news stories as well as local news and commentary. When reporters gather information on large stories, they may often wish for position papers or teaching drafts or the name and phone of a national church representative who might be interviewed on a given topic. If you give an occasional comment or compliment to such a person, you will be more appreciated when it is time for a critique of some story. The whole matter of the "referral system" and networking with colleague and community leaders is both a source of information and help and must be cultivated to the fullest.

G. *About Yellow Blinking Lights:* Great caution and care should be exercised at the outset of a new tenure. Illustrations: you won't know who in the congregation is related to whom. Exercise care. Expect that things you say will be repeated and passed on. (Therefore, it is wise to visit early on the one to five persons whom most parishioners would identify as the "elders" or the matriarchs/patriarchs of the congregation). They will appreciate your recognition of them, and they can help you with "tribal" stories, histories, family relationships and other myriad information. This is not gossip or being nosey; this is the beginning of good pastoral care. This is the "ingathering" of stories and histories. It is your beginning in "exegesis" of the congregation to grasp an interpretation of its life!

A second caution: Be careful of persons who "rush" at you in the first days of your arrival. So many various motives accompany parishioners. Some sincerely wish to extend welcome and hospitality; some had a very bad experience with the last pastor and are coming in to "size you up" and take your measure; others lost out on some proposal or decision and wish to win you over immediately; others were "outer periphery" people who long to be inner circle with the new team now forming. It will be up to you to discern and sort and wonder about who people are. Caution lights are blinking; it is a warning and careful time. Others will hold back, but they are not necessarily inhospitable; they may be ones who care the most because they know that time and settling in is the best gift you can have at a time of new beginning; others are naturally shy and quiet but may turn out to be the strength of the parish and your ministry, just not yet at the beginning. Care taking at entry is necessary. All too soon, pastoral duties begin...

H. *About Visitation:* Proceed according to how you are in control of your schedule and understand how it explodes out of control. It is somewhat of a surprise today when one hears how little visitation is being done across the church. It may be one of most enjoyable tasks in our ministry. Of course times have changed. Often we can't get through a parishioner's answering machine. Therefore, "cold calling" seldom works. The two working parent families have changed demographics and schedules. Still, when one is able to make an appointment and have a visit, how many people express thanks and gratitude for the time and the strengthening of pastor/parishioner relationships. With attention to boundary issues and litigation, the ways of visitation have changed. Mostly, visitation to elderly/retired persons has been maintained without suspicion or caution. Some visitation to single persons needs to occur in the church office when others are around. It is helpful to think of who might visit with a pastor calling on a single person, or in a middle of the night crisis. Pastors today need a companion (sometimes a spouse will be able to go, or perhaps a pool of willing retired persons needs to be trained and enlisted for those standby crisis/emergencies which occur). The companion person may be in another room of the house making coffee or attending to other things while the visit goes on. Today the thoughts about vulnerability and even appearances of any impropriety must be considered and planned for in advance. Parish visitation generally must be prioritized as follows:

- *Crisis/emergency visitation:* Phone calls will produce "shocks" in a year's time in any parish. The sudden and unexpected death/ suicide or tragic illness will be communicated and both pastoral and congregational care moves into ministry. Conversations, prayers, meals, notes and many expressions of support are marshaled toward any person/family living through such events. Usually in a congregation such groups are called comfort or care or shepherd groups. Meals especially are so appreciated by the hospitalized, the new birth parents, the recently grieving parishioners. To be cared for in a crisis time is a mission of the church. See that it is done well; model for parishioners how you too participate in such times.

- ***"Event" oriented visits:*** These are ones that are directly connected with special events: birth and baptism counseling would be one example. A hospital and home visit are much appreciated especially in expectation and preparation for baptism. The Lutheran Occasional Service book has outstanding prayers for new births. Booklets and pamphlets describing the baptism, teaching its history and theological tradition are especially welcome. Involving members or altar guild in the preparation of baptismal napkins, candles or banners can make the event so very special. While mentioning the occasional services book, it is good to look there and reference the many and various occasions for special prayers; this book might also be close at hand for the parishioner counseling visits where there is list provided with scripture and prayers for everything that might be mentioned/confessed: depression/addiction/fear/uncertainty, etc. This is a rich pastoral resource. Take and use!
- ***Regular, structured visitations:*** Pastors will accumulate much guilt around this task because it will never be accomplished no matter what the size of the congregation. For, if you should make rounds completely, you'll want to return and begin again. This is the ministry's "never-ending tale" of good intentions. In your first year in a parish do not be bashful about making known to the parish that you will begin this process but that you would welcome calls and invitations directly from the parishioners over the next few weeks. This does a couple of good things: it informs the parish that you intend to visit, but it puts the onus on each of them to call and ask. At the time of entry into a new parish, another good idea is to make small groups work for the purpose of introduction. If there is already a small group structure available for this, use it. The concept of small groups for neighborhoods, clusters or "shepherd" groupings within the congregation is a good model for the ministry and care-taking of all

the baptized. If it is a new idea to a congregation, perhaps a council member can call and convene such groups for meeting the new pastor but also for continuing needs: information from church council, purely social times for families to get together and for meals and help when someone in the group really has needs. Such ministry is truly "up close and personal," joyous and fulfilling.

One must recognize today that the whole emphasis on parish visitation is called into question. My father-in-law and hard-nosed businessman was my first reality check on this pastoral assumption. He was a life-long Lutheran who had been in only two congregations in his 65 years. He said, "I don't expect to see the pastor in my home unless I call him (it was mostly "him" back then). "Why?" I asked. "Because he has a spouse and family who need his time and the gobs of committee and critical visits he must make at other times. A social call on me? I just don't expect it." His comments made me do some thinking about presumptions and conclusions. Perhaps this is more of a wide spread phenomena today. Certainly it varies from context to context between rural, urban and suburban areas. With mutual ministry committee and church council, discuss expectations and communicate the understandings with the parish. Many pastors wish to stay with parish visitation and not let it go. It seems especially important that new member visitation receive some priority. Here the interchanges and questions between new person (s) and pastor begins to help build a new base of relationships as both are making entries into a new place and a new people.

One of the questions we must ask from time to time about visitation is "Why are we in it in the first place?" It <u>can</u> be a place of incredible joy! Pastors are uniquely invited to come in to a person's life, to sit and converse for a while. Is it joy or is it drudgery? Depending upon you and the particulars of your life, it can be either. Let me describe three visit/conversations and illustrate how incredibly life-changing these moments can be. One is personal and is dated P.O. (that is "prior to ordination"). I was a pre-law student at William and Mary. Each semester courses had to be selected and approved by a faculty advisor. Mine was a 50+ year old law school professor. That year the college had decided to establish a religion department and take courses out of the philosophy department and give religion its own niche. I chose an elective called "Contemporary Christian Theology," and the law school advisor questioned, "Why would you want to take such a course? You must be in a church or something." "Yes," I answered, "I'm in a church." "Which one?" he asked. "Lutheran," I said. "I don't like Lutherans," he responded. "And why not?" "Because they do that confession thing at the beginning and it deflates the noble human spirit." He and I got into a hour conversation on the meaning of confession. Me, a nineteen-year-old and he a distinguished professor, enjoyed the debate. In the end he approved my course schedule with the elective and off I roamed, choosing Gospel over law. The theology course changed my life direction and interest. Twelve years later after seminary, I was called to serve in Grand Rapids, Michigan. The first Sunday a woman came up and said, "I see you went to William and Mary. Did you know my brother? He taught religion?" And it was the professor of that first religion course! He came to Michigan each summer and we enjoyed lunch and conversations. In two years his mother, a member of the Reformed Church who had been confined to a nursing home, died. Her pastor had retired and died; the chaplain had resigned and left and they asked if I would do her funeral. Fourteen years after being a student in that professor's class, I officiated at his mother's funeral in Grand Rapids, Michigan. That's the Church! The incredible Holy Spirit blowing where it will in classrooms and course schedules, in vocational re-directions, into the geography and mapping of parish life and all the way to a proclamation of the Gospel at graveside in seemingly roundabout ways. Visits and conversations and great moments can be life changing in their impact. But we only may know in hindsight.

The next illustrations come from my ministry as a pastor. One parishioner was 80+ years old. She sat up front in church and was the only woman with a hat every Sunday. I got to know her over a couple of years until that day when her family called saying she was near death. I went to sit with her. She seemed unconscious but would drift in and out while we watched and prayed and waited. I usually wore a clerical collar and did so that day too. And that was the "uniform" she would spot upon waking, while otherwise drifting in and out. "Pastor," she said, "thank you for baptizing me." (I had not). Sleep again took her. She awoke, "Pastor," she said, "thank you for confirming me." (I had not). Sleep again, then brief consciousness: "Pastor," she said, "thanks for marrying me." (I had not). The clerical collar was her reminder of a pastor's presence at every significant event in her life. (About Clerical Collars: see the attached article, appendix A, first written in Seminary Ridge Review where this story was recorded (Lutheran Theological Seminary at Gettysburg, Spring, 2001). It was not Jim Cobb she was thanking, but the long procession of pastors who had gone before. How rewarding for me (and us) to hear her thankfulness for ministers throughout her years. Our presence in special times and events is indelibly imprinted in the hearts and lives of many parishioners and it is a joy!

Certainly, we must admit that sometimes visits are taxing and no fun. What about the parishioner with such dementia that he/she seem to know no one? Must our cars stop at these places when there is more vital ministry with other people and places? One parishioner was 100 years old; it was around Christmas time. The daughter-in-law who was the caregiver invited some folks for a party and she invited those comfortable in doing so, to enter the invalid mother's room to speak to her. "Mother," spoke the daughter-in-law, "everyone is hear to wish you a happy birthday and to say Merry Christmas to you." Merry Christmas! Suddenly, the old woman burst into song in her native German language, "Stille nacht…," she sang. And there was no dry eye in the room. It is wondrous to behold a Christmas miracle.

What does one expect of visitation? Never worry about words or agenda or how you think it ought to go. Just go! The Spirit goes before you and is with you and leads and guides. You do embody the "grace of our Lord Jesus Christ, the love of God and the communion of the Holy Spirit." Your presence is the Word moving, reaching out in ministry. Visitation, all sorts and types, may be the place where our "cup overflows" with goodness and mercy all the days of our lives.

"Finally, but" most importantly (and actually as a first priority), visitations ought to be made to church council members, committee chairs, all parish leaders and parish "tribal chiefs" in order to cement the best possible relationships in parish ministry. A great test is often put to us when we journey to those people who are "opponents, agitators or problems." We must enter in to hear their stories, hurts and hopes. If they have consistently had the reputation of "alligators," the ability to listen to them early on is important. Avoid giving agreement to their gripes (often about former pastors and other parishioners), but get across the hope you have of concentrating on the Gospel trajectories of Jesus in leading this congregation. In each of the parishes I have served, some hard opponents have left the church and moved on. Several became isolated and side-lined; a few entered into respectful but neutral "truces," and a few have even become cordial (but cautious) parishioners. I remember a Bishop's assistant saying once that a particular parishioner had a history of undermining each and every pastor. But once, in a hospital crisis, the corner was turned (crisis may be a gift at times), and later the Bishop, knowing the long history of pastoral attacks by the person, heard this parishioner stand up and proclaim in a congregational meeting and "Thank God for this pastor." And everyone who heard was astonished! Yet such transformations do occur. It is the power of the Gospel. It is the unending task of visitation to build relationships with others, not for our own protections or even our own ideas, but for the "mutual up-building of the body of Christ Jesus." (And when a pastor is wrong about something, an opposing parishioner is exactly God's gift of a corrective opponent. Be humble and prayerful and reflective about such matters). May visitation be a vehicle of joy, a true means of grace for koinonia.

Questions for reflections:

1. What are your memories of entry into a new parish?
2. What initial crises did you experience and what were the resources you used in ministry?
3. How have you "boxed" with the shadow of former pastor (s)?
4. What are your thoughts about "generic" civic prayers?
5. How are you supported when you must "tip toe" through mine fields?
6. What "paying the dues" was expected of you in the first days of parish entry?
7. What visitation strategies do you use?
8. What family considerations were most on your mind with your move?
9. What are your thoughts about "opponents," opposition and treatment of those who present a constant "prayer challenge" to you?

NUTS AND BOLTS OF PARISH ADMINISTRATION:

Most pastors enter a new congregation rather naively. The hope is that an office, a council, all committees and the whole congregation are running smoothly and that all is well. Alas, reality hits. Lay people who have worked hard and have been burned out during the vacancy have awaited your arrival in order to turn over their responsibilities to the new pastor. Within 6 months to a year, the turn-over of committee workers or chairs will seem like an avalanche. It's not all you! They can't all hate you in six months (can they?), but sometimes it will feel that way. Can you negotiate an agreement that everyone stays in place for a year? If so, do it. Probably at the congregation's annual meeting there will be one-third to one-half of the council newly elected, so change is coming anyway. The reins of this wagon are being turned over to the new pastor. There is an up and down side to this moment. The "down side" is obvious: all these people have quit, and you don't know the ropes yet. The "up side" is simply a derivative. There may be new people, new energies and new ideas, but all these tasks can't be only yours nor can you begin to do the tasks suddenly vacated. It's time to think administratively and structurally.

But first a word about where it all starts: in your heart and mind. We do so little sometimes, to look inwardly to the personality, work and thought styles, and the "outlook-on-life" that is the contextual person at the center of parish ministry. There are several 'most important' traits for pastoral administration. First, is an ability to be "extroverted" when the role is called for and demanded. Since most ministers are introverted, this "throwing the switch" is absolutely necessary. Why? A pastor upon arrival in a parish is suddenly cast into the role of "authority" and of "host." Yes, the parish may have a 200-year-old history. Yes, it may be your first day, but the reality is that you now are looked to in many and various ways. Business people will think of you as CEO. Children used to mix up my last name "Cobb" and call me instead "Pastor God" but then so are all pastors (up there in front or up high and dressed in robes and speaking with and about and for God!). Many will think of you as chief religious parent! Therefore, you have a hosting role. No way around it. Will you be forever the good host? Will you model and practice gracious hospitality and wrap it all in humor? Will you, frankly, enjoy people? If this has no commitment or priority in your personal, personality portfolio, there will be a continuous struggle in parish ministry. You must, for example, stay around church for conversations and welcome and listening. (I have known pastors to exit the room or building immediately following the benediction...unbelievable!) You must soon know who is newcomer to worship and get to them before they exit. You must invite people into events, programs and ministries. You will be on the phone, in the homes, in committees and forums to encourage, cajole and affirm. You will model enthusiasm and energy or the lack thereof. You will model hospitality and welcome even to those you may not like. You will model a way of handling conflicts and disagreements with dignity. You will either major in pettiness or proclaim a larger and greater vision for the people of God. Your excitement and passion for the ministry of the whole Church is either contagious or dampening and deadly. (Yes, even denominational programs are oftentimes worthy of our endorsement, excitement and energy, in service to the whole Church). You will roam around committees, groups, luncheons, dinners, Bible studies and be the one who welcomes. Is it obligation and drudgery or duty and delight? A pastor's attitude in this one area will enhance or diminish ministry.

One additional word about the pastor's humor and self-effacement: don't take oneself so seriously. How tempting for pastors to think that their words, work and leadership are absolutely crucial to the kingdom's triumph! Not so. The Roman Catholics have a story that is such a good reminder of this. A person named Jean-Baptiste Marie Vianney (St. John Vianney) is known as the patron of parish priests. After being a deserter in the French Army, he studied for the priesthood. He had great difficulty learning Latin but eventually was ordained in 1815. He was appointed a priest in a small, remote village. Parishioners soon considered him to be uneducated and much too zealous about the faith. A number in the congregation circulated a petition declaring him unfit to serve as a priest. When he got to see the petition, instead of tearing it up, he himself signed it! Now the irony: the notice of his act of humility and self-effacement spread through villages and ultimately the whole of France. Crowds then began to come to his village and seek his counsel on various matters. In 1855, an estimated 20,000 such visitors arrived to see him. What a powerful reminder of St. Paul's words: (II Cor. 5:7) "But we have this treasure in earthen vessels to show that the transcendent power belongs to God and not to us." What does a pastor think in such moments of seeming attack? Can my failure and failing mean that I must throw my life onto God's lap alone? Will that grace be sufficient? Can I not agree with every belligerent parishioner, that I am indeed unfit for this calling? What a paradox our calling is when we realize that we strive to be the best, do the best and yet would be the first to know and admit, "I'm a joke." This must lurk in the minds and hearts of pastors, yet the blend of humor and humility is gracious and wonderful.

These things said, it's on to some practicalities...

For years parish administration has had a bad name. It is far down on the list of what pastors think is a priority. It is near the bottom of the list when congregational profiles are composed and mailed off to Bishops during vacancies. The secretive truth is this: administration is a ministry. It even appears on a list of the gifts given to some in the church (see St. Paul, I Cor. 12:28)! How about administration making the list? Yet, how many pastors fain disinterest or speak derogatorily about such tasks as juxtaposed over and against "real ministry?" What preparations for administrative "nuts and bolts" shall we identify and use? Two tools should be most obvious:

THE PARISH CONSTITUTION: If this document has been included in "call committee" packets, good! If not, get a copy quickly. First, when was the document last updated? That will say much about how a parish has stayed "current." Look to the familiar areas of the constitution but also the optional places where the congregation made its own decisions: what is the rotation and tenure of officers? How and for how long are committees formed? What are the particularities of the parish (as most likely to be found in the by-laws and continuing resolutions at the end of the document). When is the annual meeting? Who votes? What are the duties of pastor, council and congregation? What is the committee structure? How much money may be expended beyond budget? One of the sessions that the pastor and the council president and/or vice-president should have annually, is a sit down session on the constitution to ask questions about what is being done or was left undone in the year past. Based on the constitution there can be an evaluative session to check in about tasks and roles and assessments of such things. In each congregation, as congregational meetings are called, the necessity of designating a "parliamentarian" familiar both with *Robert's Rules* and the parish constitution is absolutely essential. The criteria of "good order" is a necessity that the pastor may not personally provide, but the pastor (with the Council) ought to see that that such provision is made for each congregational meeting.

THE BUDGET: After 27 years in parish ministry, a statement made long ago by a wise churchman holds true: "a church budget is the most important theological document annually produced by the congregation." Yes! Take the budget and discover some interesting things: what is hidden and what is revealed? What are the priorities of the congregation according to its resources? What percentage of benevolence/outreach moves beyond the local parish? What is the statement being made about staff/programmatic ministry/outreach? Along with the budget, summaries about the percentage of persons or families who sign 'statements of intent or time/talent commitments may be indicative of overall member support of the congregation's ministry. Also, are there special offerings, endowment/investments and if so, what are the expectations for such funds? How directive (or not) have previous pastors been with regard to expenditures and all financial affairs? Has there been a regular audit of all funds? These are some of the crucial questions upon entry into parish ministry, and they continue as on-going concerns in the parish each and every year of your leadership in ministry.

THE PARISH REGISTER is another tool of administration, hopefully not unknown but often hidden from sight; be sure to bring it out, look it over. In all congregations the parish register is a vital and legal document that the pastor is charged with keeping. It is historic and archival. It is the official roll of membership, births, baptisms, confirmations, weddings and funerals. It has entry places for elected trustees and their terms, church council members and their terms/tenures and historic entries concerning special events and observances in the congregation's life. It should be kept in a fireproof place and under lock and key. One hundred years from now someone may seek a date or a wedding or funeral anniversary, and the parish register is key. It records letters of transfers and deaths, which are the two removals from rolls provided for in many parish constitutions.

After a pastor has a good grasp about these key issues that guide the life of a congregation, there are certain hopes that one must "work at" for the congregation to live into its potential. The first can be called:

The Congregational Climate:

In my first solo pastorate I arrived in a congregation that had known a "small, sleepy town existence" until it awoke one day and discovered it was a Metro Washington, D.C. suburb. Arriving on this scene I saw that a new sanctuary had been built, but the congregation thought of itself as small and burdened and unsure of its abilities and potentials. These are the elements that turned things around:

- A softball team! You hardly consider this to be an article of religious faith? God can use any means! Let me explain. The congregation at worship had three sanctuary exits from which they could depart each Sunday. On my first Sunday there, I was surprised to turn around and have so few people to greet. They scattered to the exits. Why? No one knew each other. The average age of the congregation was 16! In other words, young families with young children made up the membership. Someone proposed a church-league softball team. This pastor (young at the time) also played. One night during a game, I could count over 70 people out and around the sidelines! Moms and children and Dads talked and laughed. Soon on Sundays, the aisles were jammed after church. The people lingered and conversed and laughed. Small groups formed around hobbies and recreation; people began to come earlier to Sunday School (for adults). They liked knowing and getting to know each other. God was granting the gift of "koinonia," fellowship in the church! And it is one of the gifts so needed by all people. We Lutherans are so teased about our potluck dinners and menu mentalities that we forget that the table in the midst of God's people ought to be mirrored by the peoples' table of hospitality and grace for each other. Our strengthening from the table upstairs helps us in the strengthening of the table downstairs and vice versa! Of course, Christians should know this. Early Christians brought bread and wine when they came together. Some was set apart for the table liturgies, and the rest was taken and given to those in need. The Lord's table and the kitchen table are related. Koinonia and fellowship are gifts filled with grace as we live among God's faithful people as an extended family of faith. Modern people may be losing the intimacy experienced in years past when church dinners and picnics were inter-generational events, but this gift and process is recoverable. Fellowship is a very real possibility in our congregations and it is the hunger and thirst of a needful world. When ministry gurus tell us that for the success of the church we merely need to find a need and fill it, here is one within the grasp of every parish no matter its size or situation. Fellowship in the "breaking of bread" is elementary and miraculous all at once!

Parish communications:

- Announcements on Sunday: Some people love them. Some hate them. Some say "Never repeat what's printed in the bulletin," and the arguments go on. Communication experts tell us to find ways to give out a message five times if we expect it to be received. What shall we do? I believe the worship of the church is the gathering of the family. The pastor and those members leading special ministries/events and programs should speak, inform and invite. This is family business and news. Certainly if we have any hope that people might show up, we must stand, speak, inform and invite. It is a verbal necessity so to do! As a visitor in parishes, I have heard too much, too long and have "been done to death." There is a middle way....speak concisely, invitingly, informatively. Different voices should be "up front." Most parishes give announcements and welcoming words at the beginning. Their placement is not so important but ought to have some agreed upon rationale. It can be "prelude" to worship. Luther gave parish notices immediately after the sermon. He saw such notices as opportunities to respond faithfully to the Gospel proclamation that parishioners had just heard. Parishioners ought always to feel that they are "in-the-know" about events, calendars and opportunities in the parish.
- A stuffed bulletin! As part of the "five times to communicate a message," I have always used any bulletin inserts provided by the church, its agencies and institutions to give information about the church and its ministries to the congregation. We are stewards of the mysteries of God, and sometimes that means that much of our ministry is hidden and unknown to the person in the pew. The pastor ought to want the parishioners to know about "Church," to know about colleges and seminaries, camps and homes for the aging, global missions and world hunger, disaster relief and the next quilting group! There are no small offerings in the Church. And the Church is larger than the globe! Keep the information flowing. Yet the pile of trash on Monday morning is a scandal as so many have dumped their bulletins and paper inserts across pews and floors. However, some of the

bulletins do get home and read or referred to during the week. What seeds are planted? A couple of years ago I picked up a magazine of one of our church institutions and saw the list of donors. There in the list of significant donors was the name of one of my parishioners whose name was a sudden surprise. Knowing that such a listing was public, I went and congratulated and thanked the man. I asked, "How did you come to give it?" He said, "Well, many years ago, the pastor here made an appeal for that ministry and I thought that someday if I ever could give a gift, I would do that." Many years ago! Was it an announcement or a bulletin insert or a sermon? He couldn't recall. But the joy of the gift and its good placement in the ministry of the church was but a seed planted long, long ago. (And, of course, I was somewhat jealous that I had since made numerous and worthy appeals in our congregation, but he chose this designation instead. I confess my pastoral short-comings....or, was he hard of hearing now in his elderly years? Or, has a seed been planted somewhere for many years hence? Do we know God's time and stirrings?)

Stewardship:

This moves us on to a wider theme about stewardship and the gifts and resources represented in the membership of all congregations...

The goal of stewardship is to find a person's niche in order that he/she may have the joy of giving. But first a word about budgets and baloney...

Whether it is a bane or a blessing, I have been privileged to serve a couple of very wealthy congregations and both had money problems, or at least, so they perceived. My first parish began with a budget of $30,000, and the next had a budget of $300,000. All the dynamics and "feels" are the same. It's just a matter of zeroes. There is no time in any congregation regardless of size or resources, that doesn't feel threatened by impending financial disaster. Why do we always seem to have treasurers or finance committee chairs who think the parish stands on the brink of bankruptcy? Not one of these congregations has yet filed "chapter 11," bankruptcy. But the worry, the energies and the concerns around the tables of such council meetings has continually been a draining/depressing if not despairing moment and, in hindsight, none of it was worth an ounce of depression! Concern, yes, depression, no. Of course, great energies must be expended toward informing, asking and encouraging the congregation in its giving. "Giving" is a principle of Christian faith. We contribute to spiritual deprivation and suffocation if we pastors fail to speak this fact. I do not mean brow-beating; I do not mean weekly crisis reporting, and I certainly do not mean manipulative, guilt producing, money campaigns. But giving and the joy in doing it are signs of healthy faith. The point was well made in a talk I heard by Detroit's Roman Catholic Bishop who had been on a government tour with a U.S. Senator in India. They made rounds with Mother Teresa and parceled out food to some persons who literally lived in cardboard shacks on city streets. When they went in one such dwelling, Mother Teresa gave the day's portion of rice. The woman thanked her guests and went to a bowl where she poured in half for her portion. After they left the Senator asked Mother Teresa why the woman had done that. "To share it with someone else," she said. "Then why didn't we leave her a double portion?" asked the Senator. "Because we must never deprive someone of the joy of giving," said Mother Teresa. This "theology of stewardship" is the one that must guide our motives in what pastors bring to the congregation. To fall off this balance beam is to crash into the "religion-on-television" appeals that we so abhor. Yes, it is good that people give; giving is modeled by Jesus; it is a mark of thankfulness; it is an indicator of one's spiritual response to the Gospel; it is the mark of a healthy steward and disciple of our Lord. Thus, it is not money for money's sake.

Part of the balance of stewardship is also known and proclaimed in the offer of our time and talents in service to church and world. Notice the last word: world. We must always understand that vocation is our service to God and neighbor. We have heard the phrase throughout our church: "ministry in daily life." Frederick Buechner's definition is best: "The place God calls you to is the place where your deep gladness and the world's deep hunger meet." (Wishful Thinking, p. 119) All the baptized are called to serve and to serve with the talents and gifts that find their "niche" in what produces our pay-check. Hopefully, this is a place of deep gladness meeting deep hunger. Otherwise, there is restlessness and wandering in a desert place and the spirit languishes. Part of a congregation's "culture" is the understanding people begin to have in terms of how their gifts and talents get identified and put to use. When I hear the lamentations of clergy about the isolation or loneliness in ministry, I wonder about their whole concept around the phrase "priesthood of all believers." We are not in ministry alone. There is partnership in Gospel, in church and in the tasks and mission of the church. The gifts of the laity may too often go untapped due to the pastor's own isolation or sense of being threatened by the leadership of laity.

To form partnerships in ministry, we must ask others for their help, both prayerful, financial and with time and talent. It is good to ask. It is good to give. The letters of St. Paul to New Testament churches show a partnership in prayers, in money and in personnel for mission. We are inter-related in mission, in all of these ways. It is no secret that when a certain TV evangelist began his major church building, the first million dollar gift came from a Lutheran in the Midwest. When someone went and asked the person why they had not given such a gift to their local parish, the person said, "Because they never asked." Parishioners have gifts sometimes so hidden that pastors or other parishioners simply do not know. There are great secretive surprises in matters of stewardship. Once upon a time a congregation was almost full of mid-level federal employees. Salaries were average to large. The largest giver in the congregation was a retired school teacher! Once upon a time a parish had numbers of wealthy persons and everyone whispered that the budget depended on these people. The largest giver: a retired nurse! As pastor, I have been in the top ten givers in my congregations but certainly not in the top ten incomes. There are ways to calculate what a tithe of a congregation's income might mean to a budget and to challenge the congregation to grow in giving. But the budget planning process is a necessity for such growth. In August all committees should be submitting plans for ministry. The Finance committee ought to review and advise and send forward a recommendation to the Council. The Council should propose a projected budget to the congregation by October (dates will vary if the parish is on other than a calendar year budget). The congregation should hear the plans, then forward pledges or commitments to giving. Then the council will review and recommend a proposed budget to the congregation. For most of our congregations, the last process will involve cuts. No congregation seems to make a proposed budget come in line with projected income. The goal, however, is process, input from wide numbers of members, from all committees so that the budget is indeed built from the bottom up. Cuts and delays in possible ministry expansions might be kept visually in front of a congregation by moving to a two or three-column budget with projects for the years ahead. (When congregations I have served have used a two or three-column budget, the ministries have not waited longer than two years to be implemented! Articulating the needs and hopes in a vision for mission is the most important matter). A pastor ought to both lead in giving and in celebrating what a budget means. It is the annually-adopted theological plan for mission and ministry. There is a point where corporate and good business thinking leaves off and faith and unpredictable hope takes over. Every pastor will experience what this means. (See Appendix B for the best summation I have found for determining a congregation's potential giving of a tithe of its income. Many "business types" in the parish will appreciate the fact that homework is done in this regard and that the congregation's potential and beyond has been considered)

THE BUDGET AND THE PASTOR: HANDS ON OR HANDS OFF? Well, the answer must be both. Surely, a pastor engaged in active, directive words about the budget will become known through the parish as someone "pushing his/her own budget." Use some common sense: hands off with regard to salaries, property and even most of the program areas where committees have had their input. But "hands on" as an advocate of benevolence/outreach. When the Scripture reminds us that "Where our treasure is, there our heart will be also," we should know that. Even congregations with small budgets should strive to see that a minimum of a tithe (10%) of offerings are given beyond the local parish. Churches will also strive to grow proportionately in such giving and model for all parishioners how the giving should be in a people of generous hearts. Sometimes, over zealous parishioners on church councils can bring forth good causes in the community which are worthy of support. Some degree of support can go forth for local needs, but I believe we must first be advocates of our church-wide ministries. Why? Three reasons: First, it is our church. There is no one else to support it but those in this congregation. Many good and worthy charities can appeal to humanists/atheists and the general public as well as various civic foundations and endowments. But the Church can only call on the Church, its own members, for its mission and ministry. Second, our denomination does a good job with our partnerships. We do not always see or know the vast partnerships we are serving in global missions, world hunger and disaster relief, theological education, social service ministries and on and on. There is a really excellent track record for missions and ministries supported by our congregations gathered together as a national and international church, which leads to reason three: indeed, where our treasure is, there our heart will be. When a congregation gives monies beyond the local, it tends to increase its awareness of where and what it is supporting. Thus, if a seminary is supported, the parish will want to read about it, hear about it, and be informed of what goes on there. If a missionaries are supported, many will want to know where are they, who are they, what are they doing and, what are their needs? In the advocacy of church-wide ministry support, the pastor realizes something very special about his/her ordination: he/she is a pastor called by this congregation, but he/she is a pastor ordained into the whole church. Sometimes, the pastor may be the only person in the place to speak about the ministry and mission beyond the parish. Pastors are leaders in this deliberation about budgets and benevolences. Do not shrink from the task. Also, make connections with the ministries supported. Most all of the congregations I have served have provided honoraria for one special guest preacher each quarter who comes and represents that ministry in the local congregation. This gives the church-wide ministry a face and a relationship that is strengthened by such visits.

Continuing with Stewardship matters: pledges and commitments of time and talent are vital to a congregation. It is our way of asking for persons to apply their gifts and talents for the life of the congregation in its service to our Lord. But there are pitfalls. Once the list is compiled or completed of who has committed to what, certain dynamics will come into play. Example one of a pitfall might be this: suppose Ms. Smith has chaired altar guild for a half century and expects to continue. Unless there is dereliction of duty, or unless a pastor wishes to implode the whole parish, there is little chance for change. Recognize and work with such "turf" territories. Hopefully, the parish constitution will provide for term calls for all officers in the parish, but committee chairs, etc., are seldom addressed in the constitution. Working with an objectionable or obnoxious person will be expected of pastors! And how you treat the onerous types, the unlovable ones, will be watched and critiqued by the parish. Tread gently and use all good people skills to work with and for and then, if necessary, around such ones.

Watch Out!

Example two of a pitfall: perhaps a person has signed up for a role for which he/she is not suited. Suppose a person is engaged in a protracted divorce proceeding and one of the charges being weighed is "abuse." Then that persons having volunteered to be a youth group sponsor will not be appropriate. The air needs to be cleared, and perhaps the Council will adopt a policy in any event that workers with all children and youth will be subject to background checks (yes, sadly, we live in that kind of world). Upon entry into a parish, a pastor perhaps will want to use an illustration or two about confidential or extenuating circumstances that might preclude a person's offer of time and talent. The pastor (perhaps with the parish President) should bring forth appointments that have been agreed upon and then ratified by the Council. The congregation should hear that the time/talent sheets are guides to one's offering of gifts, and they are honored where possible. But not all wishes are filled (for example, perhaps too many ask to serve on the same committee). One pitfall for the pastor: the pastor's discretion in appointments ought never be used as a screening of "opponents or opposition" members. Pastoral authority is truly abused when one would simply choose friendly faces. Vibrant committees bring forth differing viewpoints and handle conflict constructively. It is the model for good ministry so to do! It is a model for the whole church that wide differences are embraced. Every pastor has been known to be on the wrong side of an issue from time to time! Maintain a large vision of the church. Hopefully, your theology embraces and believes in the ministry entrusted also to the laity as the people of God. A pastor's discernment of issues and events leads in model, example and content of how something is thought through. Model it well.

Pastoral and Parish Gifts:

A word too needs to be said about an issue that looms large in congregational life: discerning what is important and what isn't. What is petty and trivial and what isn't? When there has been time to establish good relationships in the parish and when trust is mutual, I have so appreciated the insights of the laity in the congregation. Pastors get so caught up being the "movers and shakers" in parish life that active leading and doing can drain one's energies and all good sense/balance is lost. I had an associate pastor who was nearing retirement who liked to say that on occasion he would "visit the local train station in order to just watch something move that he did not have to push!" Pastors can identify with his lament. But nothing is as beneficial as a trusted and insightful disciple of our Lord who can speak the truth in love to you. In my parish experience, I had a laywomen tell me "The congregation is ready to do more than you expect of them" (it was a building program and I was in a 'cut the budget' mode). I had a layman tell me, "Preach, preside, teach and visit, and let us handle the budget and the property." And there is a nothing more liberating than a good directive word to help us divide the roles properly and understand what mutual ministry really is. So much of parish ministry is good discernment. Martin Luther often used the Greek word "adiaphora" to describe what is meant. How shall we discern what is central and what is trivial? When a pastor is asked for leadership or commentary about issues, think on this premise: what is theologically sound practice and how can I explain this? If it doesn't fit this question, it probably is a matter of your personal tastes and that will not be the same as the musician's or altar guild's or property chair! And...if there is a theological precept at work, share it, explain it, and if your lead is followed and you win on a committee vote, communicate the rationale to the whole parish. We are teachers of the faith and parish practice is guided by Christian theology. (Of course, to use it, we have to know it).

Specialties...

An additional thought on the good use of pastoral and parish talent is that it is good for pastors and parishes to find a specialty "niche." For pastors, we see this modeled in conventions or assemblies. Bishops or presiders must rely on persons who are "specialists" in various ministries. So when the time on the agenda comes, a person speaks about the seminary or the college or the camp; another speaks of ecumenism, child and youth ministries, agencies and institutions. Each has a specialty. A professor in seminary was the first to propose this model. He said, "Pastors will become the last of the "general practice" folk. And while that is good and proper, every pastor might also consider becoming an expert in one thing." We don't often organize around this principle except in de facto ways. In the ministerium or conference groups, there are various roles which one assumes. There is one who is a fairly good Greek or Hebrew scholar (but not the rest of us!). There is one who is up on church-wide issues/politics and concerns. There is one who is interested and adept at counseling, another who is current on community needs and interests. And we need each other just this way. What a good gift and contribution to share! And it brings up one matter of great import to pastors: get into a group and enjoy it! When a new colleague arrives, the welcome should be special. Finding out about the new pastor's "niche" can benefit everyone and should be welcomed and expected. When a new pastor begins with a group and drops out, it's a cue to watch out. So many "lone ranger" types will predictably get into trouble without the lifelines of colleague support. I feel so fortunate to have been in clergy groups (usually Scripture study groups) who have an agenda to study the upcoming texts, but who often diverge into the "problem de jour." Such divergence will drive an agenda-oriented pastor over the edge, but most of us need to relax and understand that a group's purpose is not always its purpose.

Likewise, a congregation might do well to develop a "niche" and be known for some one particular thing in the community. As a newcomer in a community, ask some businesses in town or down the street what the congregation (called so-and-so) is known for. See what the response is or isn't. Only large congregations or the phenomena called "mega churches" can be so-called "full service" ministry churches (usually meaning a gym, a stage, concerts and a bus). But every church can and is special in God's kingdom. I once had a parishioner confined to bed who said, "I'm not much good for anything, but I can pray for people and I can make phone calls." She did both so well that her ministry was integral to the congregation. Another aged retiree said, "I can give you Monday mornings in the church office." And she wrote personal, hand-written notes to visitors which were so special to our guests. We have moms who car-pool neighborhood children to choir practice. One woman had hand-sewn over 250 quilts for Lutheran World Relief. One retired couple became resident experts on world hunger and the church's disaster relief ministry. One retired teacher signed up with global missions and taught English in China for two years. I am constantly amazed, and so should we be, at the ministry, the imagination and the wonder of it all in God's hands. Congregations have potential niches: soup kitchens, youth ministry, choral/instrumental concerts, adult education; there is a place and opportunity to specialize and lift up a ministry that can be celebrated with wonder and joy.

IT'S A COMMITTEE SO WHAT DO YOU EXPECT?

My wife and pastor colleague has a great phrase when she often says we help to "make ministry happen." Ministry does not "drop into one's lap." Ministry is not even simply "reactive" to circumstances and conditions. Ministry comes through prayerful planning and thoughtful reflection. We have both sat on church council where a committee chair has said, "We have no report." But did they meet? There may be a time with various holidays when a meeting does not happen. What does a committee do? What is a committee for? Every group will have some conflicted personalities at work in them. Those who know the "Myers-Briggs" personality inventory will understand that there are some "J" people who are extremely agenda oriented, task oriented and business driven. Others of us are like "P" personalities who don't care if there is an agenda or if anything gets accomplished. We tear up lists, but we love to reflect, probe and think reflectively. Here are the ingredients for explosions! How does one find a balance? Ought not committees discuss personality types in first meetings so that there is a handle for humor and gentle "ribbing" of one another when you're eight months into the year and the wrestling between the "types" has begun? Obviously, the church would hope that some tasks and good works can be accomplished, "Lord, help us to do something for God's sake!" But how about meetings when there is no task or agenda? Is not study and reflection also a worthy work? I think, for example, of worship and music committees. An agenda might have task groups reporting: acolytes and servers, choir, altar guild, greeters, lectors, ushers, assisting ministers. And a committee might go for weeks with agenda task reporting. But would they ever learn more about worship e.g., history, traditions, theology and planning for Advent, Christmas, Epiphany, Lent, Easter, Pentecost? The balance of tasks and reflections is a delicate walk at best. And how about the relationships of people on a committee? Is that not purposeful and good? I think committees should meet monthly. Tasks are important, yes, but in the months when there are no real tasks or agenda during a "quiet time," work on the nurture and growth of committee members. What a novel idea! There is so much information about every area of the church's work that an hour devoted to an article or a book or ideas from other churches can be invigorating and refreshing. What is your idea of a committee's purpose and work? Deal with differing personalities; balance times between tasks and learning, and enjoy the presence of one another as co-workers in the ministry of our Lord.

Questions will often be debated about the number of persons on the "ideal" committee. Much depends on the numbers and availability of members in the congregation. Much can be said, however, for attempting to have committees around the same number as the congregational council, if the membership is large enough to support that kind of quota. Some would argue the opposite: the smaller the better and more efficient. If a committee is task-oriented or agenda driven, then of course, smaller may be more efficient. But I have always considered committees to be a part of the small group ministry of the church— that what is most important is a "niche" for every person. With an appointment there comes a sense of appreciation and, hopefully, ownership for the decisions and work of that ministry. In such a setting the task or agenda may <u>not</u> be the main thing. More important will be face-to-face relationships, friendships, and especially, education. A committee ought to have study time as part of its composition. The leaders who can explain why this work is important and why it is Biblically or theologically grounded in the life of the congregation will be much appreciated (except by the "J" types who want to get work done!). In such a setting a chairperson should be training and rely on a partner called the vice-chair. The comittee, by its non-task driven agenda, makes people want to come, want to be contribute and results in satisfactions beyond the work. Such ground rules as educational moments or personal sharing time must, however, be understood and agreed to by the majority. Realize that some agenda and task oriented persons may quit. The style, size and shape of a small group can make different things happen.

AND THEN THERE IS THE MATTER OF DECISION MAKING IN THE CHURCH...

I admit to remaining rather naïve about this and yet naivete may be what is called for. My naivete and insistence in the church is that decisions be made where they are supposed to be made. If a committee is empowered and entrusted to decide on something, let it be done. If the congregational council is the place of all decisions, let it be done.

BEWARE: Many congregations operate on a two-tier level: the public place may merely be a cover for the decisions that are made elsewhere—some family's kitchen table; some restaurant in town, the church parking lot after the meeting. Often this means that the congregational "power brokers" have not been elected but will still call all the shots. Such methods are ultimately terrible for the congregation because they undercut authority vested in the publicly elected council members of the congregation. And these congregations will be the most difficult for a new member to find a "niche" and a place and calling to be used. Of course, use the long tenured members. They are obviously powerful people in a congregation's decision making can be useful allies or huge opponents depending on your diplomacy and people skills. Not so long after entry into a new parish, you will begin to discover who these people are. You can even be up-front about asking. Survey a few leaders and say "Who in the congregation has knowledge of the history and happenings in this congregation?" When you hear the same 3-10 names, you'll know who they are. Then the question, what to do? Use imagination. Perhaps these will be people who, although they have no current elected office, can be asked to hear your new idea. Try it out on them for their reaction and reflection, even their "refinement." Ask them, "Help me think this through." Many powerful authority figures in congregations have assumed such positions based on tenure and longevity, not necessarily because they have had the best ideas. The human principle at work is this: CHANGE THREATENS. Therefore, help them with such fears. Threatened people are fearful people, and when really scared they either drop out (flight) or they fight. I know of only two antidotes and it usually requires a combination of both: information and trust. Information/education can help the vast majority of people make good decisions. But be sure there is good quantity and quality of information to everyone charged with decisions. Trust is a much more elusive matter and may be related to how and why a pastor's effectiveness seems correlated to tenure and length of service. Be patient and nurture, if at all possible, the tenured authority figures some have called parish "tribal chiefs."

BEWARE of manipulative pastors too...

While discussing the very real "political" arena of a congregation, a word needs to be directed to pastors. While a congregation's attention needs to be directed to the public, elected people in whom decision-making is vested, a pastor may not then turn around and use secretive and manipulative methods to win a point or vote on some matter. A pastor too must model the "above board" rules that we hope are used by all. Congregational councils will detect whether a pastor has so "stacked the deck" that decision making goes on somewhere other than in the appropriate place.

About congregational meetings and constitutions...

Do you know why our parish constitutions do **not** allow for absentee balloting? It is because we profess that the church is a living body, the Body of Christ. Therefore, it is not static or stagnant but vibrant and alive! And we do two things in our gatherings: we pray for the guidance of our Lord through his Holy Spirit whom we now ask to be with us, and we gather in the Name of our God, Father, Son and Holy Spirit and thereby trust that this invocation and guidance will be dynamic in the conversations of the sisters and brothers in the faith. In other words, in such gatherings as "church decision making assemblies," one who is not present cannot be a part of mutual conversations within the family nor can they be privy to changes of motions and resolutions based on the living, present, active conversations within the assembly. An example of the static meeting is this: if I own stock, I get a shareholders resolution that is static and unchangeable and sent to all shareholders across the country. I am asked to either approve or disprove a slate of nominees. I am asked either to vote yes or no. This is static and the decision options are cast in concrete. Not so with Church. A dynamic meeting of the Body means the Spirit is present and active. A whole new idea may be born and take on life based on the mutual conversations of the members of the Body of Christ who each have gifts (charisms) that are given for the up-building of the people of God. This is the church's theology and understanding, and it is quite different from the workings of business or corporations.

(One caution though: most constitutions will allow for a wide-ranging array of matters in parish life at the annual meeting of the congregation. The constitution may also state quite explicitly that "at special called meetings of the congregations, only those motions or agenda items previously announced may be considered." This is for good order and protection. To announce one matter to the whole congregation and then allow such a "special, called meeting" to become something else, is unfair to those who are not able to be in attendance. Since every member would know of the importance and general time frame of annual meetings, thus they are very open as to what may transpire under "new business" or "other business.)"

The plea to go public and stay public in decision-making is important for fairness and for integrity as well as for newcomers who wish to be included in parish life. It is essential that the pastor insist on such understandings (however long that may take to model and make happen.)

(Note: by the word "public" I do not suggest that executive sessions are not appropriate; they are. I use "public" in the sense of the official, elected and appropriate body entrusted with decisions in the congregation as opposed to unofficial, informal, un-elected authority).

ABOUT A VARIETY OF OTHER "LAND MINES"

Or, who's got the power? Various missteps will be made by every pastor. Several however, appear over and over again. In small congregations or large, a knowledge of <u>who is related to whom</u> is practically essential to your "early warning system." Large family systems and networks can be very protective of one another and attack any outside threat (like a new pastor). A family unit may be so competitive and full of rivalries that if one says "It's a nice day" the other will object. It is good to get a lay of the landscape early and increase your knowledge and understanding of such dynamics.

About change theories...

Realize that there are two theories across the church about change. One theory says "don't change a thing for a year." The other says "make all the big changes immediately." I have seen both work. Which will you choose and why? My choice ought not be yours, but I will express it realizing that one's personality has a lot to do with the choice you make. When a pastor arrives, many in the parish come rushing at you to turn over the "reins" of this or that matter that has been waiting for a pastor. There are high expectations that the pastor take on things quickly and expeditiously. With such huge change impact underway, I always thought it best to make some major moves quickly. The rationale: to get some of them over with but always with an ingredient of flexibility. For example, when I preside at worship, I chant the liturgy. I expect that a call committee has heard me do that in the last parish and has given some notice that that is my style. (Wrong assumption. Call committees communicate too little back home!) Anyway, the first Sunday in one congregation, I will always remember that matter. Heads in the congregation were down toward the hymnal as usual when I chanted the first notes of the liturgy. Suddenly, heads snapped up like a hundred car pile-up with everyone suffering from whiplash. I knew immediately that they had never heard a chanted liturgy before. But my decision was to stay with it and offer my first courses to all adults in the congregation on worship/liturgy and sacraments. In that same congregation I had been used to standing floor level in the center aisle for informal announcements. In the huge sanctuary of the new church, however, I could hardly be seen and barely heard. The better place was the lectern with its excellent microphone. The next Sunday I used the lectern and stayed there for all announcements. Big changes, little changes and a lot of flexibility: these are the necessities in congregations. As soon as possible, however, a new pastor should bring as many adult classes together as possible to delve into a teaching ministry about the issues that you feel strongly about. It is especially helpful to give theological grounding to your parish practices that involve changes. You have great opportunity to bring people into your theological rationale for parish practice and such a forum is of great value early on.

About music and choirs...

For years choirs were referred to as the "war department" of the congregation. Sometimes the conflict is directly traceable to a director. Some of the antagonisms are deeply seeded through centuries of conflicts (Read about the factious wars between J.S. Bach and pastors of his time; it wasn't pretty). Generally, my problems with directors have revolved around three basic issues: first, a mentality about whether the choir is for performance/concert offerings or integrated for choral leadership and the under-girding of the congregation's musical offerings. This looms as a huge stumbling block between pastor and musician.

Second is the matter of what is "appropriate" for a festival or season. There may be a wide chasm of opinion here. The pastor and musician in the best of relationships might debate, explain and lobby each other for their positions but must come out of planning sessions with a united front towards committee and choir. Never should such questions between a pastor and musician be brought to public forums where votes and winners/losers will result. Staff relationships are entirely different from the "public place" of decision making described earlier. As an example of prejudices and flexibility, I remember this illustration. One parish I served had a highly active bell choir. I had a one-on-one meeting with the director. I asked that bells be banned from Lent. Their sound is joyous and festive and is appropriate for festival seasons of joy. The director however, thought that six weeks of non-performance (which is the word I have such trouble with!) would be detrimental to abilities/morale/practice and attendance. She asked if I would be open to listening to an arrangement of the hymn "When I survey the wondrous cross." I agreed to listen to a rehearsal. And I changed my mind. The bells rang forth an appealing sound that was mournful and reflective. She won her case. So did I, I think, as the director helped this pastor to broaden horizons. When there comes some impasse, and there most assuredly will be, the pastor must be and is in charge of the congregation's worship. Pastors must be integrally involved in worship planning but may give over some of the micro-management pieces concerning anthem selections, even hymn selections if there is trust in the musician's expertise. The coordination of multiple choirs in worship will be a challenge that the pastor also must arrange due to a knowledge of sacramental services and special events which may change the flow and feel of a given liturgy.

The third problem area is political. Often a dedicated choir (and we must affirm and give thanks for their commitments and dedication) can become so attached to a director's psyche that a disagreement with the pastor or unhappiness about this-or-that can ignite into a firestorm. It is the group in a congregation that sees each other at least twice a week. Strong friendships form and so do some rather hardened opinions about worship/music/liturgy and sacraments. Choirs are seldom the people of liberal tendencies. Therefore, change again, is a threat and the new is feared. Pastors in new entry situations might universally expect judgmental and rather harsh treatment for new ideas. Everything you are represents change: what you look like, how you stand, how you speak and preach and sing; everything is so different from the last pastor that the odds against you are stacked. (And then you propose to tread into their space. Watch out!) Sometimes visitation early into choir members' homes can help, but there really is a "group mentality" with choirs (check how often new members are welcomed or whether the choir is growing) that it is a hard place to be. I have no experience of great success in this area but perhaps voicing the problems will help others recognize some universal dynamics.

MISSED ASSUMPTIONS ABOUT THE PASTOR:

I have described above how valuable a mutual ministry committee of folk has been in my life. I'd like to illustrate how a parish assumption could have become a major blow-up if we had not dealt with it constructively. When I entered a new parish in Michigan, I followed a pastor who had served there for 20 years and left at age 58 when elected Bishop. After a few months of weddings, I began to see peoples' looks of frustration when I would not accept an invitation to either a rehearsal dinner or a reception. I began to ask about expectations, and the mutual ministry committee was helpful. It seems that the last pastor (male) and his wife had gone to both for every wedding. But I was the successor senior pastor at age 33 with a kindergarten child and a new baby. Both my wife and I could not go to two events but usually tried to accept one of the invitations. The couple of times we did try both rehearsal and reception, our babysitting bills were huge for the number of hours given. The committee suggested explanation via newsletter not of just one "assumption" but others about visitations/hospital calls, etc. It was a good and informative thing to do. (Notice, of course, how the committee did not recommend that the babysitting bills be paid by the church. Never expect such a solution). How surprised we were when people came around to think through an assumption and understand how the pastor's place on an age or time line varies as to what can or cannot be done in terms of schedules and invitations. Nothing else needed to be said, and it was never whispered or spoken of again. Sometimes, forthright communication helps. Pastors will need to consider when and how to communicate personal and family needs, and mutual ministry committee can be a life-saver.

Pastoral Reporting:

As leaders in congregational ministry, pastors are asked to give church council reports and annual reports to the congregation. No where in my seminary training was there a suggested "report" form or even a hint that this was expected. Most all council agenda will include such a place for a pastor's report, and through the years I have seen everything. I could point you to clergy colleagues who answer at each meeting, "I have no report," (I can hardly refrain from critiquing that answer) to several pages that read like a personal diary. (Any monthly pastoral report should be only one page or less in summary form; otherwise, it won't be read). Somewhere in between "nothing" and "everything" there is a middle way. Two thoughts about this piece: one pastor's report I saw gave the names of those visited. Don't! In a month's time, perhaps multiple visits had to be made but in a public document that calls attention to something that may be confidential. Or, maybe those visited are your best friends and you went to their house each week and called it a pastoral visit. Aggregate numbers are fine but not the names of visits. Another prominent senior pastor used a one page "critical incident" in ministry as a way of reporting— just a glimpse of an episode in ministry in the month past with no names attached. There is wide variation as to type and style.

Second, ask the council what kind of report they wish to receive. I was surprised by one council's reaction that they did <u>not</u> want numbers about various tasks included. Some council members may wish for the former pastor's way of reporting because they know of no other options. Provide some and come to a mutual agreement on the style of reporting (annually). If you do not report numbers, you will still want to keep monthly tallies for your annual report because such reporting is good information about the stewardship of the pastor's ministry and should be celebrated. (Included as appendix F is a sample report form that I most often used as one example).

COMMUNCIATIONS IN THE PARISH is another vital linkage in the congregation's life. Two things I would refer to here: the parish newsletter is an excellent means of communication and email is another. Whatever the congregation's means of communication, there are wide variations in parish newsletters. I have seen some that I thought were a waste of paper (total announcements interspersed with "devotional thoughts for the day.") The newsletter can be an important teaching tool. The pastor has every opportunity to teach about festivals, seasons, special needs of the parish, etc. A pastor's column should be the regular feature and the pastor will have to make decisions about space, content and what goes in and what doesn't. A good newsletter can cement and bond a congregation together. What is its readership? Every Pentecost festival I could tell! Annually, the congregation was invited to wear something red on this day when the tongues of fire and the red blood of the martyrs were remembered and celebrated. Look out into the congregation on that Sunday and you will know the readership of the newsletter! A second communication hope: that every parish home will have a subscription to the denominational magazine. Denominations have excellent publications and in every parish I have advocated for an "every member plan" that gets the magazine into the homes. Is it read? Perhaps we won't know, but the ministries and mission of the wider church are brought to us in an excellent journal. The readings are devotional, current issue-oriented, and prophetic in treatment of needs and hopes, ministries and missions of the Church. It helps a local parishioner know what the wider church is thinking and doing and helps with the sense of being a part of the church catholic. It is a good thing to do!

Questions for Reflection:

1. What are your thoughts about parish administration?
2. What is today's "parish humor" moment that helps you maintain a sense of humor?
3. How does a parish constitution form/inform our ministry?
4. Is the budget always the "elephant in the room?"
5. Evaluate fellowship opportunities in the congregation.
6. How do you consciously give parishioners a wider view of the church's mission and ministry?
7. What "turfs" and "tenures" must you be aware of in the congregation?
8. Do you agree with the need to have parish decisions made in the appropriate and public arena?

NEW PASTOR, NEW PARISH

SURPRISES IN MINISTRY:

People have sometimes asked me about some of the biggest SURPRISES IN MINISTRY. Let me share some. I am surprised at the number of transients who come to each and every church building in a week's time. I am sure this depends on location and accessibility, but it has been a phenomena not only during my 12 years in urban Norfolk, Va., but also in the suburban parishes of Fredericksburg, Va., and Grand Rapids, Mi. Congregations try to make every effort to be generous and caring, but pastors will be challenged to develop both a thick skin and a heart of compassion and mercy. I think over the years of the thousands of dollars in rent/utilities/medicines/food/clothing and counseling that have gone forth, and usually a parish knows little of this work of *"caritas."* Sometimes the pastor's family can be a tangential victim. Let me explain. Pastors' families most always have to figure out how to celebrate holidays. In our case, we had an early Christmas Eve worship and a late one. Therefore, the understanding was that we went out to dinner between the services. The children knew that pastor parent would come home around 1 A.M. and collapse, knowing of an early Christmas morning wake-up call from excited children. The first year the two children were both teens, they decided to wait up for us and have a fireplace and candles and food ready at the 1 A.M. arrival time. Mom and kids were home wondering what had happened. The candles melted and the food was eaten and sadly, all went off to bed. What happened was this: a transient had come to the back pew during the late service. When he passed out, the ushers got him outside to some cool air and revived him. As parishioners exited the service, he vomited on the church steps, and there was stench of urine too in his clothing. An usher volunteered to remain and help but the other pastor and I asked him to go on home to his family and we would take care of the man. We loaded him into our car, got to a shelter and it was full (like the inn in the story of that night). But the night manager said that on Christmas Eve the man could rest in the lobby. Thus we left him with shelter and provision. The journey home found the lights off and everyone in bed; a note said, "Waited till 2; sorry we went to bed; we had good intentions." Awaking at 6:30, the morning Christmas excitement began with the explanation of what had happened. I called the shelter at 7 A.M., but the man had departed into the morning air. That concluded Christmas Day's ministry. A year and a half later on a summer day, I was crossing the street from bank to Church when a man called out, "Are you the pastor here?" "Yes," I said. "I want to thank you. Do you remember that Christmas you got me to the shelter? That was me," he said. As I looked closer, saw a clean-shaven and well-groomed man, not recognizable from that Christmas night. He said, "I was on drugs and had been drinking but I got into AA. I've got a job and things are much better now. Thank you." Sometimes, it is so good to go home and tell the family about an episode's conclusion. Our frustration with the inconvenience was met by a moment of grace in a life turned and re-claimed though we had little to do with the transformation. The surprise to me in this story is not in the rescue and change; it is in the "thank you." In the thousands of transients welcomed and assisted, he is the only one I can say has ever returned to say thanks. When Jesus healed the ten lepers and only one returned, his 10% of thanksgiving is probably higher than we will ever know. Of course, discretionary funds have assisted many church members and those stories are usually wrapped in gratitude. But in the urban ministry of our cities, the church simply gives and sometimes gives out and may even give up. The ministry of help looms large, especially in our cities. Hardly anyone knows.

Thoughts on the subject are these: thankfulness will not be expressed; give anyway. Try to organize as church coalitions to make the best use of church resources. When your "compassion index" is zero, consider our Lord's continuous grace given to undeserving and non-thanking people like us! Ask for help in such diaconal ministry and consider ways that the laity can serve. Ask permission to speak a prayer for people as they leave. Their circumstances, even if 'con artists,'are hard and cruel. Try to embody grace. And remember it is "heavenly grace and delight" (and plain good manners) to be surprised when one returns thanks.

WEDDINGS would be my second greatest surprise. A few years ago I visited my high school principal who has kept up with me through my years in college, seminary and parishes. He asked, "What in ministry baffles you the most?" I think he expected me to say certain scripture texts or people's behaviors but I quickly said "weddings." Weddings confound me in two ways: people I think have everything going for them can crash and burn in a year and people I thought had little to commend to each other in this covenant relationship are faithful and steadfast and enduring in their relationship. There is no index, test, or assumption known to humankind that can foretell a verdict about a marriage. It is a mystery to me. The second and most ominous surprise about weddings is that it is my least favorite thing to do. Why? I've tried to answer that question. The issue revolves around "to whom does the wedding belong? The church or the couple? The largely un-churched or pseudo-churched designation of so many people today means that they see the event through cultural filters. Big reception with big band with big bills with wedding directors and musical magnificence and glamorous staging **<u>or</u>** a worship service of the Church and therefore guided by the faith, the Gospel and the integrity of the Church? You know which half of the possibility I endorse. There is a great deal of humor around weddings, if one can keep a sense of humor at all! I think every couple should see Steve Martin's movie, <u>Father of the Bride</u> and read Robert Fulgum's book, <u>It Was On Fire When I Lay Down On It</u> where he has a chapter about MOTB (Mother of the Bride). Such humorous treatments have a kernel of truth in them. These events too are matters of importance or "adiaphora." When a wedding **<u>is</u>** worship we invoke the Name of Jesus, we read Scripture, we proclaim the Gospel, sing, pray and bless. Therefore, texts and what they say are important. Perhaps a John Denver or Judi Collins piece can or might speak the Gospel but maybe it doesn't. And who gets to make such a call? The Pastor. My surprise is that seemingly good and faithful church women and men seem to lose all perspective and discretion when "their big day" approaches. What skills in planning are required and what diplomacy to speak the truth in love! Novel idea.

Next big surprise: (and this is one especially for seminary students and recent grads). Because we clergy are professionally trained, we have come to be at least respectful, if not over-awed, by "intelligentsia." For four years we moved through colleges and universities and were taught by learned and revered professors. Seminary faculties are much the same. Many have Ph.D. degrees from the world's most prestigious universities. Their learning is deep and impressive. They carry on research in their fields of study; they have written scholarly books and always seem to engage in erudite conversations. And their public lectures "showcase" their great knowledge, expertise and extensive vocabularies. And we all wonder if they made perfect scores on their SAT's and GRE's. At the point of graduation/ordination, clergy must beware of two temptations: the first temptation is to think that we and our scholarship are now "set apart or above" the common folk in our parish. The first five years in parish ministry we tend to bring our new theological vocabularies to the congregation and deposit our good learning on the heads of poor, dumb parishioners who don't know a chalice from a paten. Somehow, we come to think that we are truly God's gift to these people to eradicate their ignorance and uplift their learning and once people simply "know" the right theology and liturgics, all will be well with this parish. WRONG!

A second temptation is to think that all distinguished teachers must have the Ph.D. credential to speak and lead the common folk in the right discernment of truth and understanding. Now the huge revelation to me after nearly three decades in ministry is that God has turned this world upside down too! We get to ordination/graduation with our heads, while the Christian faith is experiential and "of the heart." What a moment of learning this is! I learned about evangelism not so much from any seminary Ph.D. professor but from my four-year-old son who invited his pre-school buddy to church. Then the whole family came, and we had a bunch of baptisms one Sunday. I learned about prayer, not so much in liturgics class, but in the ER room when a teenager had hanged himself. I learned about prayer from an elderly invalid woman who said, "I can't do anything else but lie here and pray for you and anybody else in the church you need me to pray for." I learn about ministry in daily life from parishioners who share with me some of their real dilemmas in their work places when questions arise about ethics, integrity, fair and just personnel practices, and the all-too-often inhumane corporate mergers that lay off a large work force.

I learn about Scripture when a layperson takes up a passage and says, "I thought about this last week when...." I've learned so much about the resurrection standing by a newly dug grave in the local cemetery. I am sure many readers know this revelation already, but for me it was quite a surprise and an adjustment. I come from a church that has long professed belief in the "priesthood of all believers," but has made the pastor the chief residential faith person. I keep finding that the God who created and called these Christians into this local parish had them rounded up and into a lot of faith arenas long before I arrived. How I have been surprised. And how the prayer of pastors really ought to be: "Lord, let me not do too much damage here. Amen."

If the above perspective is really absorbed into the persona of the pastor, a couple of things might result: first, there is appreciation for the people and their life stories and experiences as true revelatory accounts of the lively Gospel of Jesus Christ. If we do not believe that we are God's great gift, an "all wise" guru dropped in to teach and lead from outside, we might just relax and enjoy these fellow Christian disciples who are "on the way" with Jesus and with us! Humility allows for humor to be the tie that binds. These simple folks are the very saints of God! And something has happened to them: they have been baptized and God's Holy Spirit has taken up residence in their lives too. That ought to count for something! What is it? How will you listen and hear and discern such wondrous things?

Second, there will be great patience and care-taking for this people for we know we dwell with a holy people in a holy place! Yes, there may be factions and fights. Yes, there will be dissension and misunderstandings. Yes, there will be murmuring and gnashing of teeth in many and various ways. But there is a theology of the church that proclaims that this people, called in their baptisms and gathered around the word, the bath and the meal, are God's own people and the very body of Christ! Paul put up with the Corinthians, John with the Gnostics, and so it goes on and on, this marvelous people called "Church." Can we still see the belligerent one, the factious one, the slanderer, gossiper and the back-stabber as the very one for whom Christ died? Can we, who mess up ministry in so many ways, drink the grace of the living water that we too will need in our thirsty droughts of despair? That core group of 30-80 who come each and every Sunday, expect them to show up as the "saints in light." Why not affirm, enjoy and absorb them now that "they may be in us and we in them as the Father and the Son are one" and proclaim the unity of the church on earth and in heaven? Yes, such a change of perspective is called a "paradigm shift" (of major proportions!). God's grace is good to let us in on such surprise in parish ministry!

Questions for reflection:

1. What have been your biggest surprises in ministry?

2. How does this local congregation fit into your theology of church?

3. How do you think early church dynamics are repeated in today's congregations?

OTHER CONSIDERATIONS...

"A CHURCH PROFESSIONAL:" OBSERVATIONS OF A HOMILETICS INSTRUCTOR

by Rev. Dr. Susan K. Hedahl
Associate Professor of Homilectics,
Lutheran Theological Seminary at Gettysburg

Dr. Hedahl presents the following to seminary students in her preaching classes:

What characterizes the professional church leader?

1. ***Graciousness.*** You learn to speak the gospel in an inviting manner and do so with poise and confidence in your call, your Lord and yourself. You encourage the same in others.
2. *Discretion*. As you proclaim and discuss, you note the boundaries between private and public speech. Not all thoughts and feelings should be accessible to the public. A measure of personal privacy respects and protects you and others.
3. ***Restraint.*** In the pulpit or group discussion this involves thinking before speaking, deciding if what you want to say needs to be said in that way, at the time, in that place. Restraint allows you to listen more closely and receive new information more easily as you make decisions.
4. ***Appearance/Demeanor***. Preaching is an incarnational event! It is estimated that 90% of verbal communication depends on the non-verbal presentation of the speaker. Distracting matters to listeners - over which you have control - should be noted and changed if necessary. This involves wearing inappropriate jewelry, hairstyles, clothing, make-up and weight issues.

   The Gospel is attractive! And you, as its proclaimer, are to be the same.
5. ***Thoughtfulness.*** As those in theological training, true professional church leadership demands intellectual, personal and ethical integrity that reflects itself in corresponding words and actions.
6. ***Hospitality***. Preaching/living the Gospel welcomes others' thoughts, ideas, experiences, and opinions. (Agreeing with them is another issue!) Hostile, indifferent or inattentive responses on your part are unbefitting a professional church leader.

Conclusion:

Being a "professional" is not simply a matter of feeling but of acting, doing. Consider the dynamics described above as practices, formation of habits that characterize the professional leader in the church. They are marks of the servanthood ministry. They spell out the points of a disciplined spirituality.

> *"Finally beloved, whatever is true, whatever is honorable, whatever is just, whatever is pure, whatever is pleasing, whatever is commendable, if there is any excellence and if there is anything worthy of praise, think about these things." Philippians 4: 8*

I would like to make some comment on each of the excellent points made by Prof. Hedahl because I believe they are very much "on target." I like to think of graciousness as "grace-ness," realizing this is a new word of sorts. The pastor is, (whether one accepts this or not), for many, the embodiment of grace in that her/his persona is the communicator and courier of the Gospel. Yet, in a day's time, that may be a taxing and trying role. There are belligerent people to deal with who are lashing out in their anger. There are frustrated ones, homeless and off-the-street who do not know where their next meal comes from. There are persons who are mentally ill or emotionally spent looking for a listener or a counselor or a representative of God. When such persons approach, you too may be having a bad day, be out of sorts, argumentative with spouse, upset with children and laboring under a day scheduled with no breaks. In walks a person in crisis. You are God's ambassador of grace. How this role will tax you to the limits. You are, for others, an "icon" of faith. You may be the only Scripture this person will "read" and the only incarnation of the incarnation this person may encounter. It is the persona of grace extended from one who bears and embodies the Gospel and fills the ordained office with that gift. You are it, in bad days or in good.

Second, the matter of ***discretion*** is an ongoing art to cultivate. One of the single most difficult matters is the issue of what is public and private and how shall a community called "church" live in such a way that we can pray for one another and share joys and sorrows? In a litigious culture great care must be exercised. I remember a new member who had come into our church and during a pregnancy was ordered to bed-rest for weeks. Our church included her in prayers, moved meals and visitors into the home and instead of warm appreciation, she pulled back from the church. Sometimes there is a surprising reaction. Her husband's navy assignment took their family away from our parish for a few years; then they returned and immediately re-joined the parish. I had to ask, "I thought we had intruded too much before and your reaction was one that left us wondering what we had done wrong." She responded, "I had never experienced church that way before. I did not know how to react. I felt people were doing too much and too many things for us. I was either embarrassed or resentful or both. In hindsight, it was great; I'm thankful and hope to be a part of that kind of care during this tenure. Thanks."

Now that's a story with a happy ending. But sometimes we may rush at people without knowing their reaction and the lines between public and private. Generally, the simple rule must be to ask for permission. May we include your names in our public prayers? May we say something of your condition? May we share with some of our members who have gone through a similar experience? How may we help?

In the matter of ***restraint***, I think the reason for this item's appearance on the list has to do with two things that are self-protecting: first, our anger. When it is ignited, find a way and means to cool off. Any fuse that gets lit and explodes like a bomb within us is tremendously harmful. In public arenas we must exercise restraint. Second, restraint is a reminder that our first reactions to many things, are sometimes not our best. You have probably met people whose first impressions were terrible, but over time they come to be a treasured friend or colleague. These things take time. There have been many "new ideas" at committee meetings where I first reacted negatively but then came to see some merit and vision in that idea. This too takes time. All public arenas need restraint to deal with anger and to evaluate people and ideas in patient ways— especially with media, who want a quick interview for the local news, be careful! I like what the late Rev. Will Herzfeld, former Bishop and church executive in Chicago once said, "I've learned not to argue with people who buy newsprint in bulk." When Dr. Robert Marshall was Bishop of the Lutheran Church in America, he arrived at the office one day with a gaggle of reporters and camera on the church-house steps waiting for his reaction to a newsmaker approaching various church denominational offices. Marshall ducked in a back entrance, asked his staff to receive the demands and tell the press that the matter would be considered in appropriate ways.

When our church released its national study document on sexuality in the early nineties, the press called for an immediate response to the swirling controversies and wanted an instantaneous "sound bite" for the news. I proposed instead that the congregation study the document and the press would be invited to sit in on 6-8 weeks of sessions in our adult forum. Needless to say, the press never showed up. The media really does hate "studied approaches." But we are church with a studied approach to its important decisions and moments. It is good and proper restraint and serves everyone well.

Appearance and demeanor become for many people the very outstretched hands of greeting that we so hope to find in a friendly person. Around the house or fishing or camping obviously are occasions for "dress down" times. But generally, the office of pastor carries a sense of professional decorum that one ought to uphold. Across the years I have witnessed the extremes: the well-tailored three-piece clergy suit that I knew I could not afford, to other colleagues who dressed like absolute slobs. All extremes are really affronts to the people we meet. There may also be special sensitivities in rural and small-town settings (be guided by frank conversations with parish leaders if possible). The question of "civilian clothes" or "clergy attire" continues as an on-going debate according to church traditions and pieties (and I address this issue for me personally in appendix B). Sometimes pastors have developed some habits that clearly should have been intercepted and addressed through the years and some seem to need refresher courses in basic etiquette. The following are the most obvious:

Personal hygiene is a must and the use of soap and water is nearly a third sacrament! So too, is liberal usage of toothpaste and mouth wash. The portable small toiletries are useful (if used). Every clergy car compartment needs packets of the small spot removers and cleanser wipes for small clean-ups.

At meals, napkins should be frequently used whether one feels the glob of food on the lip or chin or not. Consider that a spot of mess has landed on the lip, cheek or chin. Don't wait for a spouse to signal the clean-up!

Liturgically, hand-washing needs to happen after "passing the peace" and before the sacrament. Bowls of water on the altar once were provided for this (so that is a good historical idea still to do!) or slipping out to a close restroom during offering/anthem works. This hygienic practice also needs to be done in parishioner's homes or nursing homes or hospitals whenever the sacrament is prepared and the table is set. Pastors should consciously change hands with one used for blessing children (the hand on the head blessing or sign of the cross). It is rather terrible to see fingers move from greasy head to loaf of bread—sorry, but it's a fact). Paying such attention is worthy of our consideration.

Finally, there are various idiosyncrasies that we all have and our attention towards the annoying ones may be worth our while: it may be chewing fingernails during meetings, rattling change or thumping fingers or nasal snorts or saying "ah" in every sentence. Attention and elimination of annoyances are appreciated. How's your personal inventory and what needs attention? Who loves you enough to tell you?

We see the Gospel is indeed attractive when the clergy embodies "thoughtfulness and hospitality." At the beginning of this conversation, we spoke of the implicit role given to clergy when we are looked to as the "host" or "presider" of parish events. This we must be! Those of us who are by nature shy and introverted and would rather not host must be transformed into that role for the sake of gracious welcome in our faith communities.

When Dr. Hedahl's observations continue with the two items called "thoughtfulness and hospitality," there has been coverage in the preceding pages to detail and illustrate these necessities. One's emotional sensitivity in group settings about who is bothered, disturbed, silent, pre-occupied or upset may be important cues for follow-up. Remembrance of known anniversary dates, birthdays, death of a spouse or child can be inserted in personal calendars as reminder both for your prayer and perhaps special attention on that particular date. Such thoughtfulness and hospitality are greatly appreciated and represent ministry so full of love, grace and compassion. These "gifts of the spirit" are meant, not for our keeping, but for our giving away. Do so!

Questions for reflection:

1. Take the checklist and use it as a mirror for your reflection about yourself. Can you be honest in self-assessment? Use the list for personal prayers as you embody the Gospel to other people. Think/pray about these things:
   - graciousness
   - discretion
   - restraint
   - appearance/demeanor
   - thoughtfulness
   - hospitality

"PRIESTHOOD OF ALL BELIEVERS"

is a phrase from the Reformation which remains one of the most explosive concepts in the Christian Church. While there is great vision of Christians who carry and embody the Gospel in their "Monday worlds," we also have a potential gold mine in the church as well. There are priestly duties that one must learn to share with "fellow members of the body of Christ." Billy Graham once was asked what he would do first today in a mission congregation if he was just beginning a pastorate. He replied that he would gather a small group of people and try to teach them the things he knew and ask their help in the ministry of the Gospel. Does this sound familiar? Was this not what Jesus did in gathering the 12? So, why is this not the most obvious starting point? Most pastors get some helpers "on board" immediately. The "priestly" tasks are these: representing the Gospel to the world and bringing the world in prayer to our God. When any person catches on to this, interesting things happen. We are all able, gifted and called to this ministry in our baptisms. In the Lutheran baptismal service, the pastor announces this: "Through baptism, God has made *these new sisters and brothers* members of the priesthood we all share in Christ Jesus that we may proclaim the praise of God and bear his creative and redeeming Word to all the world." And the people respond, "We welcome you into the Lord's family. We receive you as fellow member(s) of the body of Christ, children of the same heavenly Father and worker(s) with us in the kingdom of God." (Lutheran Book of Worship, p. 124-5). As pastors, we must remember that our helpers, fellow priests, live with us and around us and ought to be invited into significant ministry. At a minimum, visitation and fellowship are tasks of the Gospel that need energies and attention. Some can write prayers. Others speak or sing publicly; some teach and administer; some have business skills and acumen; some are communicators, some friends and listeners. Pastors must lift up and encourage what every congregation needs and welcomes and find a niche for the release of these gifts.

One pet peeve: I loathe the way many churches use the word "volunteer." How many announcements and appeals and bulletins ask for volunteers? My baptism into Christ was **not** my volunteering moment. I was enlisted. I was called, chosen, set apart. But I don't remember volunteering. Also, "volunteering" seems to carry the idea of optional participation. I might volunteer for this or that, but the church needs me and you and each of us! The "body" is incomplete when any of its people are MIA's. In fact, we need to say this about worship, learning and serving. We either strengthen or weaken the body by our presence or absence. Let's play with our language a bit further....we are not to be MIA's; we are not "POW's" but we are "POC's, (Persons of Christ)." So, a POC on your house and on your church. We "persons of Christ" will serve in any way we can, give as we can, love as we must, lead when we can, and try to say "yes" more than "no" to our church in the course of a year.

One of the most important issues you will face is the teaching/rationale you will give to people about why worship. Why should a Christian give priority to coming to worship? Sociological studies would find that people come together when it is personally fulfilling (meaning that they know and love the people and the congregation and they experience church as their home). Yes, church is relational. And we know (sociologically speaking) that people who show up also give ("Where your heart is, there is your treasure"), so every church wants to increase attendance. Of course! Psychological studies would tell us that many come to "fill up" their emotional/spiritual needs. Haven't we all heard someone say, "I come to church to re-charge my batteries?" All of these "good" reasons are heard and spoken, but there are theological reasons as well. Perhaps we should speak them. My spouse told this to our children and I think it is most direct and accurate: "You go to worship because Jesus expects it!" Done, finished, answered….no more whining, complaints and deal making! Jesus said, "Where two or three are gathered together in my name, there I am in the midst of them (Matthew 18:20)." That is enough reason to come together in worship. It is our obedience to the promise of Jesus. There are also these reasons: the Holy Spirit has taken up residence in the Church of Jesus Christ. The Holy Spirit brings to remembrance all that Jesus has said and done. When we are baptized, all of this comes together in a marvelous way. One by one, Jesus makes us his Body, the Church. In English, we have a marvelous word: "remember." Add a hyphen: we re-member the Body when we come together. Members come again together to form the One Body, the Church. We come together "sealed by the Holy Spirit and marked with the cross of Christ forever." The parent (s) and sponsor (s) stood with the child and said, "I promise to bring to the services of God's house…" Such "bringing" set in motion holy habits, born now of obedience to our Lord's command both to "remember the sabbath and keep it holy, and "where two or three gather in His Name, he is there" and because when we gather, "we do this to remember him," (word and bath and meal). We speak a "body language" quite unique to the Christian Church. And the body is meant to be full and all present and accounted for. "Absence" diminishes and weakens the body. "Presence" builds up and strengthens. If you want to re-play the difference this all makes: compare the church's worship between Easter and a Sunday in August. Get the drift? When the whole body is present, what a witness, what a strength, what a joy! And conversely, when the body is diminished, what sad commentary, what a missing of the sisters and brothers who are absent, what an empty place we can see and know.

In one of our congregations, a person new to the church revealed that he had once spent some years on a taxi squad (not quite on the team but a reserve, ready-to-go group) for a pro football team. He was huge in size. He had been used by the team and then thrown to the side before any real money or pension support came along. With injured legs that didn't work and an appetite that couldn't be adequately fed by the low paying labor job he now held, he was mightily discouraged about life and people. He asked one day what good was he? I was quick to answer that any athlete was nearly idolized by kids. By being in the pew on Sunday, kids noticed. His gift, by his presence in worship, was a witness that someone big, strong, a good athlete was a follower of Jesus Christ! That's a powerful witness by his presence and participation. And as we get to know more about people, each, in whatever station in life, is a witness: the intellectual, the political leader, the public school teacher, the store clerk, the traffic cop, the medical worker. Each is a witness and our children do see and know and notice. Why would we not be gathered together for worship each Lord's day?

Jesus invites us to be there, expects our presence so that his presence proclaims the Good News, announces forgiveness, empowers our witness and our serving, feeds us bodily with his gifts, and sends us forth with renewed mission. That's the Spirit.

Questions for reflection:

1. How do you explain or interpret our call to be a worshipping people? What are the sociological, psychological, spiritual and theological trajectories of this call?
2. What have people told you about why they worship?
3. What if we are "members one of another?" What difference does this make in our lives, what are the implications?

JAMES G. COBB

MOST EXCELLENT CONGREGATIONS:

In a Lilly Foundation study by Professor Paul Wilkes at the University of North Carolina, Wilmington, a listing was made of the 300 most excellent protestant congregations in the U.S. (for a full discussion see, Excellent Protestant Congregations, Paul Wilkes, Westminster John Knox Press, 2001). My wife and I served as a clergy couple pastoring one of the congregations on that listing. We are thankful to have been a part of such a vibrant parish as First Lutheran Church, Norfolk, Va. With various similar studies there seem to be conclusions that "excellence" in congregational ministry will at least include the following:

1. A clear sense of vision and mission
2. Welcoming of innovation and change
3. Spiritually alive
4. The ministry has a sense of excitement about the future
5. New people are easily included
6. Conflict is understood as a "given" and is dealt with openly.

We were housed in a gothic church, not so popular as an architectural design today. We had a "high church" liturgy each Sunday, not so popular according to surveys today. We were "sacramentally" centered which defies many studies about church growth and methodologies about how to grow. We worshipped in a style using pipe organ and rather classical music which is not supposed to have appeal among many today. We were engaged in shelter, food and community ministries. We had an excellent Sunday Church School with more adults than children in attendance. We had outstanding children, youth, campus and young adult ministries. We led our synod in benevolent giving and we kept two missional (but sometimes orphaned) emphases on our screen: global missions and theological education. And with all of this, we grew! Defying studies, trends and advice, a liturgical/sacramental church grew; we grew in membership, in worship attendance and in giving. When I look at the studies of excellence in ministry, I believe this congregation indeed touched all six characteristics.

Relationships within the congregation were born of mutual respect and trust. Hospitality and welcome embodied by the pastors was contagious throughout the membership, and people who visited returned with the commentary about welcome and reception. New members were approached quickly about their gifts, their niche and how they would serve Jesus with their sisters and brothers. Expectations were spoken: each was expected to worship, to learn, to serve and to give. We were a highly transient membership and expected innovation and change like the rivers that flowed through Tidewater Virginia or like the waves that relentlessly pounded the shore. There was "excitement and aliveness" and energy all around. Differences of opinion were expected, encouraged and welcomed. A former seminary president was once in a congregational gathering and asked a circle of members, "What is the best thing about your congregation?" Some said the building, some the program, some the staff, some the outreach; but he was most impressed when one person responded, "When you join this church you don't have to bear anything by yourself anymore." Everyone needs a meal now and then, a friend now and then, a phone call ever so often, an invitation to go somewhere special, an inclusion with the group on an outing now and then. When the New Testament encourages us to share one another's burdens, the ministry of Jesus for us and through us to others is the discovery of a great treasure! This treasure we have in earthen vessels. Earthen vessels are plain, ordinary and utilitarian. So is our humanity. But God so loved our human-ness that he gave his only begotten Son.....

May our humanity, our human-ness, our ordinariness be the offering we give to our Lord. Each person needs a place, a word of encouragement, a welcome. Each needs a home. The Church of Jesus Christ is that place, that word, that welcome and that home. These good and common and ordinary things are the very stuff of miracles and wonders and treasures from God to us. The Church is a wondrous place and people in every way.

Love the Church, cherish it dearly and serve it in love and integrity. Give to its needs and honor its mission to raise before all the world, the One who is Lord and Savior of all.

The prayer for people and pastors and congregations is that we might be faithful to Jesus, our Lord, in all we say and do.

Questions for reflection:

1. What is your theology of church? How do you understand and articulate "church?"
2. What do you think about the six categories in common with "most excellent congregations? What others would you add?
3. Are there strategies locally, to help each category come alive in my congregation?

CHURCH FIGHTS/FIGHTING FAIR:

The obvious first: all fights are destructive, demeaning and finally, are about power (who has it and who doesn't). Church fights are particularly awful because of painful hurts, harbored resentments and long memories. At one's entry into a parish, many dynamics may already be in place from long-ago arguments, fights, or as the church likes to call it, "falling out." When one has conversations (early) with judicatory officials, raise the question about parish conflicts, past and present. Has an interim pastor been able to help resolve conflicts? Have judicatory officials waded into the fray? You will need to know this. Will a call committee be honest enough to air its dirty linen? Will church councils let you in on "closeted conflicts?" Perhaps yes, more likely, no! An outside observer could soon comment on "who will not speak with whom" in the pew or at the coffee hour, during the dinner or in a committee meeting. You may observe persons who will not pass the peace with a neighbor or who will jump to another line for communion. Yes, indeed, incredibly, that happens. God alone will be able to sort out some of this. Given that church fights are sometimes the most vicious and given that many Christians will say, "I left the church because I could not believe the fights," what are we to do when caught in such matters? The answer must be: grab onto the Gospel more firmly than ever. Only the resources of the Gospel can be an antidote to Satan's playground. We ought not be surprised that the church is a battlefield while it too is a people of peace-making. Martin Luther said, "Where the church is, there the devil pitches a tent." The Gospel's resources are these: forgiveness, reconciliation and new life. Practically, how you work that out in personal and professional strategies will vary greatly from place to place. I will share some personal journeys.

In each of my parishes (and I don't know if this is just me or whether others too will resonate with this) some member of the call committee has left the church, usually in the first 18 months. Two reasons appear to be standard:

1. They were already becoming inactive and some wise persons in the church thought if they were given a key and major responsibility it would help retain them in the church. Wrong!
2. Their sole purpose in serving on the call committee was to be sure to get a pastor on board who closely resembled the last one. Wrong!

In either case, you, the new pastor, really can't help that you are not like the last one. When I caught on to such discoveries, my strategy was this: a personal visit/appointment to try and give hearing to their problems/concerns (often not truthfully offered) and the sharing of this dilemma with a trusted colleague and/or an elderly or wise or very trust worthy member of the congregation. Usually, the feedback is: they have a chip on their shoulder, can't be pleased or reconciled; you probably need to let them go. I have experienced this in each parish. I wish they could stay. I wish there was some resolution. I even wish we could declare peace and be friendly, but it won't happen. The last pastor was their special friend. Somehow, your very presence threatens their memories, their former turfs, friendships and confidences in that pastor's "inner circle." Some circles in the congregation will be astir when such a one causes a problem. They might need to be left alone. They may leave on their own. But life will go on. Let it. Good advice.

Second, there are matters of personal dislikes that simply cannot be overcome and are a mystery to the human psyche. You may simply remind someone of another person they dislike. The transference problem has little remedy. It may be your body size, the look in your eyes or how you comb your hair but, whatever the reason, some simply will be aloof and angered by your very "being." Let such "cloudy characters" blow through like yesterday's weather front. There is no way in the world to get a grip on such ephemeral matters.

Third, most pastors meet real opponents to the ministry and the God we represent; persons whose problems are so buried in their own hearts that the real issue may never come out. This can be a matter of what psychologists call "displacement." Their anger is directed at something else but comes out in inappropriate ways. Let me create a character as an example. Doug is 62 years old and is viewed as one of the "pillars" of the church. He is consistently elected to a congregational office. His serving God is related to church leadership so this he conscientiously does. He has begun to be an opponent to your every idea. You have tried to listen, converse, invite him into plans and ministries, but he keeps undermining, complaining and going his own way. His independence is laced with a very different understanding of Scripture. You would rather he not be a leader. What's going on? From a counseling perspective, Doug needs some understanding. His personal history may be "key." He has been a life-long church member. Not so long ago a traumatic, personal crisis occurred. What's going on? In unresolved anger, he can't hate God. But Scripture, he believes, must be clung to like a life preserver. He has decided to be its literal defender. Along comes a pastor who obviously misunderstands such truth; a pastor who is such a harbinger of change. Now both his unacknowledged anger towards God and a crusade against a pastor (God's representative?) merge, and you are the target! That's displacement. Only a therapist with years of work could peel the layers from this deep wound. Our understanding and compassion wish to do no harm to the person in his vulnerability, but he needs to be proscribed in his spheres of influence in the parish, the next focus of attention.

ISOLATE AND SEPARATE is a theory and practice which is sometimes needed in the case of a severe opponent. Most congregational officers have term limits to their positions. Term limits are helpful in the necessary turnover needed in congregations. To know you will be without a disgruntled member in a year or two is almost bearable. Terms of service and rotation of duties is a good and healthy practice for all congregations. Pastors, who by personality try to please and avoid conflict, find themselves particularly susceptible to avoidance of confrontation. In my ministry, I admit to having "danced on egg shells" and tried every way possible to work things out, to use an "isolate/separate" strategy when needed, but some confrontations cannot be avoided and perhaps ought not. We pastors think we are basically likeable people and we cannot understand why someone would not be our friend. In one particular case, a parishioner was a constant source of criticism and complaint. I discovered he was the source of so much "stir" in the congregation that others who had often defended and tried to explain his actions to me came and said that I needed to intercept this person and go face-to-face. That is a hard moment for me and perhaps the reader too. I remember my own nervousness at the meeting. After some attempts at welcome into the office, I got right to it with the introduction about not being able to be like the last pastor in style or focus. And then I said what was on my mind: "I know from various people that you are the source of criticism and complaint. I hope when you have those ideas and thoughts that you will come to me directly. I'll sit with you and explain anything I can. But here's the thing: you have to decide whether you are going to assist the ministry during my time as the pastor or whether you are after my resignation." The bluntness of that sentence hung in the air as he back pedaled and stammered. He was "found out" and this confrontation laid it open. I think he was a bit startled at directness and confrontation. We now had new ground rules. He knew that I knew the source of much complaint. We never became great buddies, but a kind of truce did begin and remain through my tenure. I was very uncomfortable with that kind of conversation, but in the days and weeks after that I felt a sense of relief and liberation. I would hear later that it also emboldened other parishioners (the ones who had come to me in the first place and let me in on who and what was going on) who took a cue that confrontation towards honesty and openness can work and they were empowered to intercept his criticisms with dispatch. These moments, thankfully, were rare.

RESTORATION: In each of the congregations I have known the "opponents/antagonists" who have not exited the congregation but who have re-entered relationships with me and others and have done so admirably. This raises an issue for pastors: every opponent ought not be "blown out of the water" or "blown off" or "summarily dismissed," out of sight, out of mind. Whether they are wrong or you the pastor are, the church has great capacity for repentance/restoration work and there must be a time and patience for the possibility of such moments. And they do happen. In each of the parishes I served, I have known someone who made a personal attack or led a factious "charge" eventually come around and repair the breeches! This is good and necessary and will occur. The door must be open for this to happen. I know many pastors who have slammed the door shut on such persons. This is regrettable. Instead, there can be work at forgiveness, reconciliation and new life. Our Gospel themes can effect change and transformation. The feelings and emotions may not be "warm and fuzzy" but the opportunity for mutual respect, dignified differences and reconciliation can be a tremendous modeling for parishioners who will know and observe how you, the pastor, treat people. Some opponents have become friends (albeit cautious always), but mutual respect and deepened understanding through such difficulties can and does occur. Always keep such possibilities in mind.

Other pastoral learnings for me have included the following:

1.) Let go of pettiness. Time and energy expended on "small" things is draining, demoralizing and not worth it. Slights do need forgiveness and hurts do need reconciliation. Your heart has to want this instead of revenge or domination, but it also takes two people to want it. There is great degree of pettiness in congregations. We ought not let it pile on. Discerning important matters from trivial (adiaphora) is a constant call in the church. Let pettiness roll off and don't absorb it.
2.) Stay above reproach in your own words and actions. If you mud wrestle, expect to get dirty. We don't need to sink to the level of words, behaviors and whining that typify so many of the sisters and brothers who complain. In this sense, we <u>do</u> need to be above it all.
3.) Since active and strong opponents are constantly your "piggy back riders" through such a time, can you consciously pray for them and about them and will not this continue to be a means by which you wish them well (not ill) and by which you struggle to understand and have some measure of mercy and compassion? Often we cannot go face-to-face to simply be verbally slapped or hit again, so can they

be given over to God's care? Sometimes we must let the disgruntled ones go, leave the church, pull out of the parish. Prayers may be our only recourse, but it is a good and proper means to care for them.

4.) Stay "issue centered." Pastors really can suspend opinions about paint colors and budgets and bills and let others make decisions. Feelings and sensitivities may come to no amicable resolution, but are there issues in which the pastor's lead and guidance is indispensable? If so, lead, teach and guide. If not, there must be room for decisions.
5.) Pastoral authority must be derived from teaching authority via Scripture and theology. Yes, we baptize; yes, the pastor counsels and plans and administers; no, the council may not suggest using sand or motor oil instead of water to baptize. Yes, we do commune; no, it may not be suggested that we drop it for a year! There are issues where our Scripture/theological authority is resolute. How we discern what is and isn't important is the key and, around such issues, the congregation may thrive or dive.
6.) Trusted colleagues are a source of much needed help. Ask for confidentiality in such groups. Use a brief "case study" methodology and have various ones be the sounding board for the dynamics of your parish "prayer challenges." Insights, strategies and simply speaking the problem or naming the person can be a tremendous relief and freedom for you. You will re-enter the arena soon and your respite of alternative ways can be your lifeline.
7.) As things "snowball" and begin to loom large, you may need to share with a pastoral counselor or judicatory officials about what is transpiring. These trained persons need to detect "early warning signals" about tough situations. We should share and seek counsel and let the circle of helpers expand.
8.) You will win some and lose some. That is a fact. When you've lost a motion or plan in the council, how will you receive such a loss? Can God be working through the council to tell you no? Yes, the Spirit is as much in and with them as it is in and with you. In the field of parish life, "wheat and tares," the *corpus mixtum* of the church is a fact. God alone can judge, sort and separate out. Do you pout, threaten, intimidate opposition? Shall it be a learning experience or will a defeat spiral one down into a black hole? Others will watch and learn from your reactions to opposition and defeat.
9.) When you are despairing, get back to what is central to the ministry: Scripture, preaching, visiting and the Sacraments. In one of Martin Luther's tense stress-filled times, on the eve of a momentous public debate, how did he spend the time? Was it in prayer, or Scripture study or research about early church fathers? He visited an old parishioner, heard his confession and served the sacrament. It still

> works! Visit the elderly shut-in parishioner; sing, pray, read and serve and the clarity and renewal of the Gospel will be a gift and a refreshment to you in a time for trouble. This just plain works. Do it!

There are some fine books and pamphlets about opposition types within the church (antagonists, ankle-biters or whatever they may be called). Read some of the resources and studies. Know you are not alone and that the particular thing you're going through has been well traveled by others. The prophets were stoned; our Lord was crucified so can't we even put up with a blip of trouble? You may detect in the New Testament that Paul was most fond of the congregation at Philippi. They were generous in their giving. They were partners with the wider church in its ministries. They were helpful in many ways in their care-taking of the apostolic mission of the church. We can detect Paul's true affection for this bunch of Christians who seemed so solid and complete in their Christian faith. But then Paul had the Corinthian bunch as well. There were intense factions: some belonging to Apollos, some to Cephas, some to Paul. There were rumors of incest, drunkenness and additional listings of problems and troubles, yet Paul called this bunch too, "the saints of God." And he continued to try to help in straightening out the mess, one thing after another. And he kept on preaching and teaching about baptism and communion. And he did what we continue to do: preach, teach, visit and administer the sacraments. Good for him. Good for us. Both clarity and refreshment come to us in our attention to the means of grace.

Questions for reflection:

1.) How did St. Paul deal with various parish problems? What were they?
2.) Can you share a case study with colleagues about a tough situation you have lived through?
3.) How does one show pastoral care and concern to an opponent/enemy?
4.) How do emotions affect you and/or your family? What outlets are there for your anger, frustrations and misunderstandings?

JAMES G. COBB

PASTORAL MINISTRY LIFE SAVERS:

In my generation of pastors and among those younger in ministry, three phrases have appeared in our vocabulary and have became realities for us in ways not true with our elders. The phrases are "mutual ministry" (referred to earlier), "peer groups" and "mentors." All are life savers for pastors! In each parish I have served, the study group or the conference meetings have served as the places of "mutual consolation of the brothers and sisters." With seminary providing good and useful models in collegiality, the patterns live on in ministry. Often a group would have as its intended focus the study of next week's lectionary. In reality, the texts themselves seem to open onto parish problems, situations and crises for which the group could offer reflections, similar experiences and good counsel and advice. It takes a bit of time for the newcomer in the group to assimilate. Like all relationships, there are some pastors (sorry to say) with whom I would not choose to share personal matters. In most instances, these pastors were not solid members of the group and their dropping in and out signaled their pre-occupation with other things. For the rest of us, the absolute priority of weekly attendance was an inviolable covenant we had with one another, so very helpful and precious for sanity and counsel and consolation. (I smile in remembering one particular pastor. In one of the synods I served in the largest congregation and perhaps carried the most demands in terms of time and crises. But this pastor in a small parish always had the newest gadget—a beeper, then cell phone, then computer day calendar. He would arrive late (mostly infrequent in attendance) because of some emergency and most always get a call or beep that he had to answer immediately. I felt sorry for his calendar bondage. I wished he could be "free in Christ" to give some attention to his sisters and brothers in ministry. But he always came with the answer we all needed or the wisdom he wished us to have at his "early departure" from our groups). From such experiences, I have learned that we must both beware of and pity the "lone rangers" among us. These wish to be complete unto themselves. Such ones truly "graduated with wisdom once-upon-a-time" and have little or no need for companions on the way to reflect, pray and share. The rest of us consider the peer group and/or the mentors to be heaven-sent life- savers. Such groups and conversations bring these gifts to us:

- a safe place to explore any circumstance or situation. (The group should covenant about confidentiality and never violate the covenant. Newcomers should be introduced to the covenant).
- a chance to speak the hurt, the trouble and the turmoil. (Getting it out and said is so important to the healing and the resolution).
- an opportunity for others to share their insights, experiences and strategies that may indeed help us on our way.
- a sharing of readings, referrals or resources that we have found use-

ful in our similar journeys.

- a leading on into prayers, confession or blessing that can be spoken/ enacted either as a group or with a selected colleague as pastor (e.g., liturgies of welcome/god-speed/life changes/celebrations/joys/ sorrows, etc.).
- an exercising of a larger collegial ministerium for the care-taking of congregations through knowledge of each other's places and issues of ministry.

On the other hand, some groups are not at all appealing to the new pastor and these reasons tend to center around two matters:

- lack of welcome and hospitality and initial care-taking of the newly arrived pastor and,
- a tone of negative griping, whining and complaining that permeates the group and signals a waste of time when one is drawn into such attitudes. Also, the need to brag or "justify one's own self" before one's peers with "success motifs" is particularly unseemly.

Both of these negatives take some work to identify and get some changes effected. We've all been in such "poor me/why me sessions" that we want to shout: get a grip, get a life, grow up or deal with it! Pastors in such a group need to see and hear this critique and be accountable to make the changes necessary to transform negative to positive, and to give strength and appeal to peer groups. In parish ministry there are only four reasons to miss the meetings of our clergy colleagues:

- geographic isolation
- sickness
- out-of-town
- parish/parishioner or family true emergency

In matters of ministerial health and well-being, "mutual ministry, peer group and mentor" are realities that grace us with a peace that passes all understanding. These are pastoral life-savers and pastoral life lines. Grab on, hold tight, be safe.

A Second category of life-savers is the matter of time management. Clergy know that we are not in a 40 hour work week. Given that long hours do exhaust and deplete the human body and psyche, what shall we do? Fortunately, early in ministry, I was helped by a seminar designed for denominational executives and senior pastors of large congregations. It was a system informed by the corporate business world. The learning went like this: think of a 40 hour work week patterned for most factory/labor workers in the U.S. But instead of 40 hours, think of it as morning and afternoon "blocks" (or 10 blocks to the work week). Now look at your week's calendar: there are 21 blocks in a week: morning, afternoon and evening. How many did you work? Forget hours...if you did some parish related "work" (e.g., driving the car while thinking of your sermon but nothing else that afternoon, count it anyway as one block). How many? The leader had us look at our calendars and most had worked 15-18 blocks in that week. The numbing news was this: while most of the work/labor force works 10 and that is healthy, most managers/professionals work 12-14! And if I remember the correlations correctly, 15 was connected to stress/burn-out; 16 to health problems and 17-18 to suicide. What a revelation! Conclusions: there must be some rest and leisure time built in to each pastor's week. Our 'day off' sometimes isn't that at all! Take the blocks needed to be a spouse, a parent and a rested, re-created pastor! Engage a council or executive committee or mutual ministry committee with such an awareness about work and rest and realize that during a two-week emergency, funeral, crisis- driven week in Lent, that you owe no apology for not showing up one morning or playing golf one afternoon. (Of course, call in and explain the time off.) Also, particular sensitivities in rural/small town settings will take some special attention with regard to how the pastor's time is understood as "on" and "off" duty).

This understanding of "block time" has made the most sense to me and is as easy to figure as a quick glance at your appointment book, last week, this week and next week. Figure where the blocks are for spouse, children and you!

A third category of life saver is the whole issue of what was called "continuing education," more recently re-named "lifelong learning." The change in terms is good. How many times have pastors told confirmands, "This isn't a graduation, this is a beginning of your deepened faith adventure." At that moment a bishop should be at our shoulder to ask, "And when was your last continuing ed. course? Congregations have become mindful and generous in contributory time and money for annual study opportunities. Every seminary of the church, every camp of the church, every synod, regional, national and international expression of the church offers such opportunities. Every pastor must stay fresh and stay fed. Both are needed through a lifetime of ministry. The church makes scholarships and grants available, and every encouragement is given to promote lifelong learning as a part of a vital and growing maturity in ministry. The Scripture we read and others books too, as well as distance learning, chat rooms and internet communities we form will offer great expansion of our minds and consciousness in the years to come. But one thing will still be a lifeline for us: face-to-face relationships within our worshipping/learning/serving communities. Go face-to-face in classrooms with teachers, lecturers and presenters. Take a course in a field totally different and unrelated to your work. Audit some course at a near-by college. In a planned cycle, look to the seminary for refresher courses in various fields, but become a lifelong learner. This too is pastoral life saver.

Questions for reflections:

1. What are your thoughts about (and critiques and appreciations) about peer group?
2. How do you structure and concern yourself with time management?
3. What is your plan/strategy for lifelong learning? (name both hindrances and encouragements to such plans).

At the beginning of this reflection, I commented that this is not a "how to" book but a number of pastoral reflections of this pastor's journey. There are other conversations to have and other parish matters to explore. "Entry" into a congregation is but the beginning place, truly a "commencement" in ministry. A concluding thought from the Sarum Liturgy, 13th century, England:

> *"God be in your head and in your understanding.*
> *God be in your eyes and in your looking.*
> *God be in your mouth and in your speaking.*
> *God be in your heart and in your thinking.*
> *God be with you at your end and at your departing." Amen.*

APPENDIX A:

CLERICAL COLLAR: GIFT AND SIGN

— Dr. James G. Cobb, Pastor, Assoc. Dean for Admissions and Church Relations, Lutheran Theological Seminary at Gettysburg. (re-printed from Lutheran Theological Seminary at Gettysburg, Seminary Ridge Review, Spring, 2001)

There are many more critical issues facing the Church than this one! How shall we faithfully and devotedly preach and teach the Gospel? How shall the world hear the Gospel of Jesus Christ? How shall the Sacraments be administered and a world catechized concerning Gospel, Bible, doctrines and teachings of the Christian faith? How shall the Church minister and respond to a world whose needs are legion?

In the light of such pressing mission, of course, a clerical collar is adiaphora! So too then are books and budgets, bricks and buildings, crosses and ornaments, stained glass and statues, organs and instruments, vestments and voices, flowers, candles, pulpits, lecterns, offices and orders, and shall we also say: water, bread, wine, cups, plates and offerings? Of course, Jesus alone is the way, the truth and the life. But our Lord graces us with wondrous embellishments of creation like colors (of sunsets, clouds, water, leaves, flowers) and finery of materials, nourishment through the arts and Gospel mediated through specific means like water, bread, wine, crosses, pictures, and yes, even vestments, collars and the office of ministry!

Having said this, I know what has most bothered me about clerical collars over the years: they have seemed "hierarchical" rather than egalitarian and, therefore, a symbol against the "priesthood of all believers." And some pastors use the collar in a way that promotes aloofness or even arrogance. Such use is anathema to the Church. Also, some have so absorbed the collar as "identity" as to be laughable. I've seen pastors wear their clergy shirt and collar while pitching a softball game. You just want to scream "get over it," or more correctly, "get out of it."

Historically, of course, we know about some origins of our garb: "Clerical or Roman collars of Lutheran, Roman Catholic and Episcopal clergy is a stylized version of the neck cloth worn by all gentlemen into the 19th century," (The Encylclopedia of Religion, Vol. 3, Mircea Eliade, Ed., MacMillan and Co., New York, 1987, p. 545) and Philip Pfatteicher gives these points: — clerical dress beginning in the 4th century made a distinction between everybody clothing and vestments; special dress for the clergy outside the church building did not exist before the 6th century; black has been the color of the dress of clerics since the 17th century and in the U.S. the third plenary council of Baltimore (1884) required Roman Catholic clergy to wear the Roman collar outside the house. (A Dictionary of Liturgical Terms: Trinity Press International, Philadelphia, 1991, p. 32). Enough history…

I have also learned the richness of the clerical collar as gift and sign. Luther Reed wrote years ago, "Clerical attire is generally appreciated and respected. "The cloth," like the uniform of a police or military officer, is an indication that the wearer is "on duty." A minister, for very good reasons, may decide not to wear clerical dress at all times." (Worship, Muhlenberg Press, Philadelphia, 1959, p. 289). My children taught me about the "on duty" part of the collar. They were children in the age of *Mister Roger's Neighborhood* television. As he came on the set each day, while singing his theme song, it was to go to the closet, hang up his work/suit coat and slip on sweater and sneakers. Likewise, my children referred to "Daddy's work shirt." With "work shirt" Daddy was pastor, without it, he was Daddy. They learned this quickly, early and precisely. And I was grateful! It calmed some of the screams for "Daddy" from the pew of the church on Sunday! A p.k. learns what it is to be "on duty" and "off duty" according to the work shirt or something else.

Also, the context of my last parish taught me about uniforms' and on duty. First Lutheran Church, Norfolk, Va., was a military town. In that setting the parish and community knew that uniforms designated a job and an office recognizable in the public arena. There was no need to explain or uphold either the idea or substance of what one wore as clergy. The context of ministry was understanding, sympathetic and even expected.

Still today, the clerical collar is a "passport" garb that allows us to cross the borders of protected or prohibited places. I, like many of our readers, have experienced the "entrÈe" into hospitals, emergency rooms, funeral homes, jails, city offices, schools, etc. where a wave of the hand has signaled my permission to enter when others (even civilian clothed clergy) have been detained. For that reason alone, the collar is helpful to ministry.

My real lesson about the "office bearing" symbol of the clergy collar came from Nellie McCauley. At 88, she lay dying in her bed at home. I was attired in clerical collar as she drifted in and out of a coma. She woke, saw me and said, "Thank you for baptizing me Pastor." (I had not). She woke, saw me and said, "Thank you Pastor for confirmation." (I had not). She woke and said, "Thank you for being at my wedding Pastor." (I had not). Nellie taught me. It was not Jim Cobb she was thanking but pastors who baptized, confirmed, and officiated at her wedding. The collar represented, across time, the church's ministry. That was my second year in ordained ministry, and Nellie gave me the resolve to go forward into the lives of other people in the years to come wearing the collar to help others attach significant memories to the long steam of ministry with those who fill the office of Word and Sacrament ministry.

Of course, sometimes wearing the collar can be a problem/embarrassment. In Norfolk at a gas station across from Old Dominion University, I was filling the tank when a young man ran from his own car and asked me if I was a priest, "No," I said, "I'm a Lutheran pastor." "Same thing," he said. Suddenly, there on the pavement, he took my hand, knelt on his knees and said, "I have something to thank God for. Can you hear my thanksgiving?" I glanced around the gas station awkwardly and off guard, wondering if I was on candid camera. I mumbled "Yes." And he said what he was thankful for and ran back to his car, leaving me to wonder who and what was that all about.

The collar is a magnet for people, stories and issues. Sometimes it is a bother. All of us put it aside to have our personal time, time off, time with family, spouse and kids, and we should. To wear it is to be brought to the confessional with total strangers; to be asked to listen and help; to be approached in anger, confusion or hope (or thanksgiving?) by a whole host of people in our world. It, therefore, always means going public with our office of ministry. It means, when we wear it, that our very identity is understood not as Jim Cobb but as Pastor, a Pastor of the one, holy, catholic and apostolic Church. It is to the world gift and sign of history, tradition, apostolicity, catholicity, Scripture, Gospel, Jesus and the gift of the ordained office of ministry for the church and for the world!

Adiaphora? Yes. When the bishops of Gaul, introduced the use of new ritual garments, it prompted a stinging rebuke from Pope Celestine I (c. 425): "We bishops must be distinguished from the people by our learning not by our dress, by our life not by our robes, by purity of heart not by elegance…" (op. cited, Eliade, p. 542). Adiaphora? Yes. But the uniform of the Church simply carries too much valuable freight to be dumped. I do choose to wear it when "on duty," when serving Word and Sacrament ministry, and when serving publicly in the church and world. Isn't the point to grace the attire and to grace the office with the grace of our Lord Jesus Christ? May our clergy be worthy of that calling to which we are called. Think on these things…

APPENDIX B:

(A very interesting exercise to compute potential congregational giving. This is of unknown attribution but a very useful tool).

HOUSEHOLD INCOME EQUIVALENTS:

Number of communing members who are single and who have full time employment: _____

Number of couples (wife and husband) who are both communing members and one or both have full time employment: _____

Number of married individuals who are communing members but whose spouse is inactive in any church and where there is one full income in the household _____. Divide by two and insert figure on the right: _____

Number of married individuals who are communing members but whose spouse is active in another church and where there is a full income in the household _____. Divide by three and insert figure on the right: _____

Number of communing members/family units with limited income: retired, divorced, prolonged illness, etc. _____.
Divide by 4 and insert figure on right: _____

Add right hand column to total the number of household income equivalents: Total: ____

Find the average household income from local chamber of commerce statistics. Average cities and counties represented in the congregation or use the highest.

Multiply HIE number times the average household income: Total membership income: ________

(Note: full-time students/military personnel, etc. outside community are not counted for this formula).

APPENDIX C:

10 COMMANDMENTS OF PASTORAL "VACANCY ETIQUETTE."

1. Thou shalt not ask thy former pastor (s) to perform any pastoral functions. Such functions belong to the pastoral "office" within a congregation and not to individuals.

2. Thou shalt not complain, gripe or gossip about the changes underway.

3. Thou shalt forever suspend the phrase, "We've never done it that way before."

4. Thou shalt not sit around thy house nor thy neighbor's house nor thy relative's house and forever reminisce about the "good ole days."

5. Thou shalt not covet thy neighboring parish's pastor.

6. Thou shalt take up thine own responsibility for tithes, offerings and work assignments within the ministry of thy congregation now and forevermore.

7. Thou shalt behave prayerfully toward those taking up the tasks of ministry in the days to come.

8. Thou shalt not wander aimlessly around other congregations if thou lackest attention or leading roles once bestowed upon thee.

9. Thou shalt speak well of thy leaders and fellow servants of the Lord.

10. Thou shalt in all things, seek the good of the Church that all may be well with thee in the Kingdom of thy God.

APPENDIX D:

CHECKLIST FOR PARISH ENTRY:

(things to be done upon entry into a new parish; prioritize according to your instincts and local conditions):

- ❑ Crisis/emergencies (***priority!)***

- ❑ Council Pres. introduce you (and family) on first Sunday, welcome with reception; have Pastor introduced to each Sunday School class...children, youth, adults.

- ❑ Staff relationships: time/time/time to sit down and get to know staff, their jobs, hopes, disappointments, etc. Schedule time later to review position descriptions.

- ❑ Membership directory/pictorial directory, for names/addresses/phones/emails

- ❑ Moving in issues: books/files/office
family: spouse/schools/sports/recreation
personal: license/tags/insurance/doctors/dentists, mechanic/repair people

- ❑ Office procedures/staff: office hours, messages, home/office, cell phone, answering machine, etc., secretary/bulletin/newsletters/phone/messages/on call coverages/etc. Council President/treasurer/exec. Committee or whole council

- ❑ Contact Bishop/Dean & Council re: installation service/reception/luncheon/dinner, etc.

- ❑ Hospital: list of parishioners
  how many/where/what hospitals
  hospital: parking/entry/chaplain?/orientation/lists of parishioners, etc.

- ❑ Shut-ins: list of members/addresses/phone numbers
  beginning visitations/home communions

- ❑ Visit denominational neighbors (ask about pericope studies, conference meetings)

- ❑ Check with local courts to determine procedures, if any, for officiating at weddings (policies/requirements vary from state to state; also, check if you officiate in another state).

- ❑ Visit close-by/neighboring clergy (ask about ministerial assoc. meetings/task force groups)

- ❑ Build referral system: from clergy: counselors/food-shelter-assistance/support groups, etc (rolodex/computer reference files for you and secretary, etc.)

- ❑ Visit to community leaders:
  funeral home director (s); mayor or commissioners/ police/newspaper editor or religion writer/school superintendent or principal/college Pres./Dean or Chaplains, etc./shelter or cooperative ministries directors.

- ❑ Visitation of parish "elders" for history/context stories and perspectives

- ❑ Visit Church Council members

- ❑ Identify "helper people" for visitors ID and follow up, office and worship helpers, good "grapevine" people for news and information about the parish

- ❑ Guest appearances at committees, Bible studies, Shepherd/Neighborhood groups/circles, youth ministry, etc.

MONTHLY EVENTS/PLANNING GUIDE FOR THE CYCLES OF PARISH LIFE:

(add your own unique parish calendar items as you live the cycles and keep an overview of the coming year. Add church-wide and synodical emphases):

Jan.: Bishop's and/or parochial reports due
Congregation's annual meeting (or move to the month designated by constitution)
Lenten Planning (schedule of special services, parish mailings, buy ashes/palms, candles)

Feb.: Holy Week planning
Easter planning (Lilly purchases, etc.)
Shut-in communion schedules

March: Choosing/ordering VCS materials
Continuing Ed. Plans for the summer

April: Pentecost planning (geraniums, etc.)
Confirmation planning (gifts, customs in the parish, etc.)
Synod assembly plans/voting members elected, etc.
Planning for Summer worship/Sunday School schedules

May: Teacher appreciation
Choir/Staff/Worker appreciations
Special summer planning (picnics, etc.)

June: Fall SCS curricula/teacher appointments

July: Rally Day planning
Class listings for all Sunday School students with ages/grades for children and youth
List high school seniors beginning college (care packages, prayers, recognitions, etc.)

Aug.: Preliminary budget planning
Preliminary Stewardship planning
Fall Bible studies
Contact all confirmands about plans

Sept.: Reformation planning

Oct.: All Saints/Thanksgiving planning
Council nominations and calls

Nov.: Advent/Christmas shut-in communions
Advent planning (wreath, manger/candles)
Christmas pageant planning; Poinsettia orders

Dec.: Annual reports by all committees/staff due
Basking in Advent/Christmas worship
Planning for family time and vacation days post-Christmas

Other matters to be determined for dates/plans: first communion plans, new member classes, pre-marriage plans, ordering of supplies, council retreat/planning, etc. Other:

APPENDIX E:

CONGREGATIONAL CHECK-LIST FOR "WELCOMING A NEW PASTOR"

(by James G. Cobb, Pastor, Assoc. Dean, Church Vocations and Lifelong Learning, Lutheran Theological Seminary at Gettysburg and based in part on the book "Being a First Church," by Mark E. Yurs, Wipf and Stock Publishers, Eugene, OR, 2003)

ISSUES AROUND PREPARATIONS TO RECEIVE A NEW PASTOR:

- ❑ pray for the new pastor (and family)
- ❑ write them a note anticipating their arrival and extending your prayers and welcome
- ❑ have a pictorial directory or picture album to which all have given a picture, address, phone and note of welcome
- ❑ be sure understandings have been reached about parsonage/housing... (always consult pastor/family for their choices...)
  - ❑ (if parsonage), painting, repairs and updates
  - ❑ (if housing): are arrangements complete for settlement/arrival date, etc.
  - ❑ (give list of reputable repair persons for car, furnace, plumbing, roofing, etc.)
- ❑ good interpretation to the congregation of pastor's chief work: reading/study/preparation and immersion in the Word for preaching and teaching; sacraments and worship leadership; pastoral care, parish administration; and connections to the wider church in serving

ISSUES AROUND MOVING DAY:

- ❑ workers/helpers needed for packing/unpacking?
- ❑ child care needed?

- ❑ food preparation through the day for helpers?
- ❑ pantry shower for the pastor/family
- ❑ consideration of "start date" but allowance for a week of "settling in" needs

ISSUES AROUND FIRST SUNDAY:

- ❑ introductions and welcome hosted by congregational president
- ❑ reception or meal of welcome
- ❑ name tags for everyone (for weeks or months or permanently depends on size of the congregation

ISSUES AROUND INSTALLATION:

- ❑ careful listening/coaching by judicatory officials and newly called pastor
- ❑ writing and submission of local newspaper article
- ❑ special worship preparation: choirs, musicians, etc.
- ❑ reception planning/sending special invitations to area clergy/churches/judicatory officials and special pastoral family and guests
- ❑ offer homes or beds for out-of town guests
- ❑ help with meals for guests of pastoral family over the weekend

ISSUES AROUND THE FIRST WEEKS:

- ❑ parish drivers to give the pastor and/or family tours of the area (where parishioners live, where stores, schools, banks, doctors are, etc.)
- ❑ parish guides/drivers to hospitals/nursing homes and funeral homes
- ❑ introductions to area clergy
- ❑ conversations about parish visitations (what is expected)
- ❑ series of "welcome pastor" events hosted by youth, choir, fellowship groups, Sunday school classes or committees
- ❑ meetings with each committee to dialogue about practices and traditions and hopes for change as agenda items in each arena (especially worship, in order to know practices/traditions especially around festivals)
- ❑ plan a "celebrating traditions" event for story-telling about the history and hopes of the parish
- ❑ list some "encouragements": ways the congregation will via notes, words, calls, etc., encourage, affirm and appreciate the pastor (and family) in the first year's life

UNDERSTANDINGS (HOPEFULLY KNOWN AND SHARED BY THE CALL COMMITTEE TO THE CONGREGATION):

- ❑ finances: compensation package is completed and affirmed before arrival
- ❑ encourage the pastor toward involvement in clergy pericope and peer groups and church wide involvements for their spiritual well being

- ❑ encourage both formal "lifelong learning" events and full use of "day off" and vacation time each year
- ❑ agreement on style and substance of "pastoral reporting" to church Council (i.e., are there alternatives to "statistical reports?")
- ❑ wedding and funeral policies
- ❑ how will critique/criticisms be handled: (recommended: face to face with Pastor and parishioner; mutual ministry or pastoral relations committee?)
- ❑ Prayer concerns: enlistment of elderly and shut-ins who will pray for members concerns; write notes or make phone calls as able to assist the Pastor.
- ❑ Pastor will decide appropriate format to teach classes early on in the tenure so that all come to know and hear his/her theological perspectives

WHAT THE CONGREGATION SHOULD KNOW:

- ❑ a grieving process continues to be underway. the pastor (and family) has lost its comfort of place, people and routines to come to this new place
- ❑ the congregation may continue grieving for its last pastor or last situation of special relationships as well.
  GRIEVING takes time and has special dynamics at work: BE PATIENT; BE KIND; BE CALM; BE APPRECIATIVE of GOD'S GIFT OF a NEW CREATION NOW UNFOLDING!
- ❑ loneliness sets in because of these factors and new excitement and adventure may mask this for a while, but a time of "crash" does come when one misses friendships, routines and comforts of the past place and people, so year one and two will involve therapeutic transitioning for both congregation and pastor (and family)
- ❑ Pastor's work is not subject to a time clock. A 24/7 life is a matter of trust beyond regulation. "Crisis time" is balanced with "flex time" which does allow the pastor to serve also as spouse and parent in a life style of loving relationships…a good model of ministry. Encourage this!
- ❑ Petty criticism stings terribly and may seem trivial unless such matters accumulate in a way that becomes burdensome, deflating and ultimately depressing. Pastoral stress from burn-out to depression is a factor in pastoral ministry that demands attention. Likewise, spouse and children are subject to much of the same "disorientation" of a new move. Use their names (not "pastor's wife or husband or children); they are people in their own right. Extend friendship but allow them space and choice to find their own place and people and attachments without jealousy or resentment).
- ❑ Prayers of the congregation matter. It is helpful if one says, "We prayed for you….(time and place)." That's powerful!

APPENDIX F:

(An example of a monthly pastoral report but may be negotiated with your council)

(Use a title of your choosing, I used):

"Sharing Joys and Sorrows"
for the month of __________/year______
(always keep a report to one page)

A listing of three to six brief paragraphs or bullets of the past month's highlights or concerns in ministry.

If statistics are requested, use something such as:

- sermons preached
- worship services led
- funerals/weddings/baptisms/confirmations
- classes taught
- home visits (numbers only, no names)
- hospital visits
- counseling sessions
- wider church/community involvements
- other involvements you wish to mention (i.e., youth/young adult/senior groups, fellowship events…)